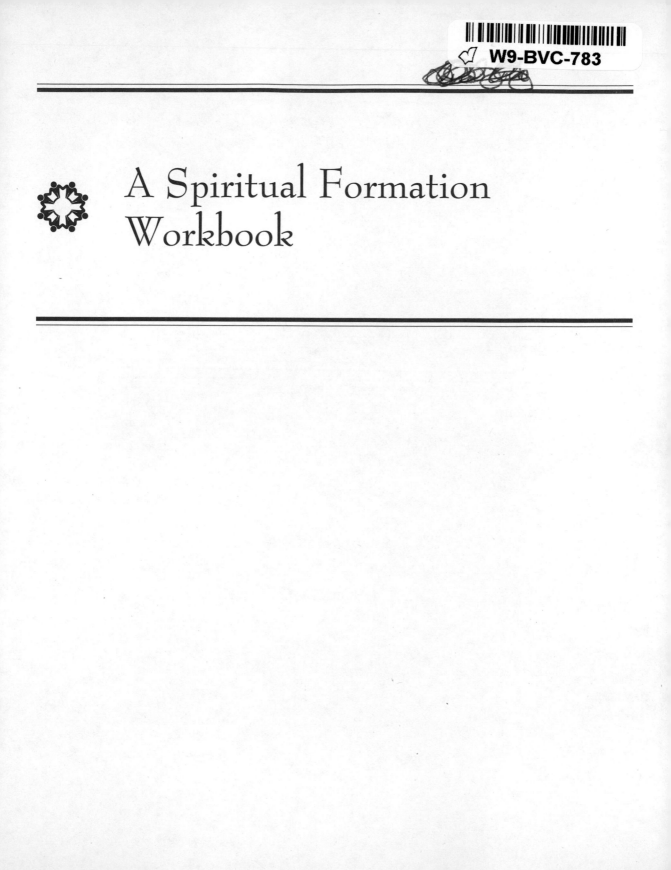

A Spiritual Formation
Workbook

A Spiritual Formation Workbook

SMALL GROUP RESOURCES FOR
NURTURING CHRISTIAN GROWTH

James Bryan Smith

FOREWORD BY
Richard J. Foster

A RENOVARÉ RESOURCE FOR SPIRITUAL RENEWAL

HarperSanFrancisco
A Division of HarperCollins*Publishers*

For information about RENOVARÉ write to RENOVARÉ, P.O. Box 879, Wichita, KS 67201-0879.

Library of Congress Cataloging-in-Publication Data

Smith, James Bryan.
    A Spiritual formation workbook : small group resources for nurturing Christian growth / James Bryan Smith ; foreword by Richard J. Foster. — Rev. ed.
      p. cm.
    ISBN 0–06–066965–9
    1. Spiritual formation. 2. Church group work. I. Title.
BV4511.S65 1993
253'.7—dc20
                                        92-36860
                                           CIP

94 95 96 RRD (H) 10 9 8 7

To my parents,
Calvin and Wanda Smith

Special thanks to: Richard J. Foster for the concept of the Five Traditions, his friendship, and his insight into the nature of spiritual growth; Lynda Graybeal for her oversight of this whole project; Virginia Stem Owens for her expertise in line editing; Greg May for his wonderful initial graphic design and icon illustrations; Kandace Hawkinson and the people of HarperSanFrancisco for their belief in RENOVARÉ; my wife Meghan for her support and encouragement; and all of the Spiritual Formation Groups everywhere whose feedback was an essential part of this effort.

Contents

Foreword   ix

Introduction   1

Starting a Group of Your Own   5

SEVEN BEGINNING SESSIONS   11
Becoming a Spiritual Formation Group

Session 1   **Discovering a Balanced Strategy for Spiritual Growth**   13
The Life of Christ and the Five Dimensions of the Spiritual Life

Session 2   **Discovering a Life of Intimacy with God**   20
The Contemplative Tradition

Session 3   **Discovering a Life of Purity and Virtue**   25
The Holiness Tradition

Session 4   **Discovering a Life of Empowerment Through the Spirit**   32
The Charismatic Tradition

Session 5   **Discovering a Life of Justice and Compassion**   39
The Social Justice Tradition

Session 6   **Discovering a Life Founded upon the Word**   47
The Evangelical Tradition

Session 7   **Discovering a Practical Strategy for Spiritual Growth**   *54*
                 The Spiritual Formation Group

                 Periodic Evaluation   *61*

                 Ideas and Exercises   *65*

                 Order of Meeting   *77*

                 Weekly Worksheet   *81*

 # Foreword

For some time now I have participated in two Spiritual Formation Groups, and I continue to be immeasurably enriched by both experiences. The first group is composed of only myself and one other person—the author of this book. The second involves myself and three other individuals.

In the fall of 1988, Jim Smith and I started meeting just to see how a nurturing fellowship of mutual accountability might work. I cannot tell you how encouraging and fun those first meetings were: we laughed at our foibles and rejoiced in our successes; we prayed; we made confession; we brought the grace of forgiveness; we made mutual covenants; we challenged and encouraged one another. They were high, holy, hilarious times.

In time Jim and I were led to study many similar small group movements such as the Benedictines in the fourth century, the Franciscans in the thirteenth century, the Methodists in the eighteenth century, and Alcoholics Anonymous in the twentieth century. We also began developing a balanced vision of Christian life and faith and a practical strategy for personal spiritual growth—and much more.

The second group came a bit later, but it is equally encouraging and hilarious. Why am I in two groups? I guess because I need double the nurture and double the accountability!

Briefly, let me explain why these Spiritual Formation Groups mean so much to me.

First, I like the sense of community. None of us is supposed to live the Christian life alone. We gain strength and help from others.

Second, I like the nurturing character. The rule for our weekly gatherings is a good one: give encouragement as often as possible; advice, once in a great while; reproof, only when absolutely necessary; and judgment, *never.*

Third, I like the intentionality. Our purpose is to become better disciples of Jesus Christ. Everything is oriented around this single goal.

Fourth, I like the loving accountability. I need others to ask the hard questions about my prayer experiences, my temptations and struggles, and my plans for spiritual growth.

Fifth, I like the balanced vision. To be baptized into the great streams of Christian life and faith helps to free me from my many provincialisms.

Sixth, I like the practical strategy. I want and need realistic handles that actually move me forward into Christlikeness.

Seventh, I like the freedom and the fun. These groups encourage discipline without rigidity, accountability without manipulation.

I enthusiastically recommend this workbook to you. It is the fruit of extensive study and research into group dynamics and the nature of spiritual development. It also has the ambience of those early meetings Jim and I had together. And, you know, we are still meeting . . . and the times continue to be high and holy and hilarious!

Richard J. Foster

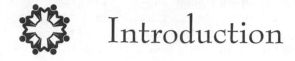 Introduction

WHAT IS RENOVARÉ?

RENOVARÉ (a Latin word that means "to renew") is committed to the renewal of the Church. It is an "infrachurch" movement. RENOVARÉ is an
effort focused on the renewal of churches, not an institution designed to re-
place the Church.

RENOVARÉ provides individual churches with a balanced, practical,
effective small-group strategy for spiritual growth. The aim of the program
is to give depth to our desire for God. The end result of the program is a substantial increase in the level of discipleship. While it is impossible to measure spiritual growth, those who have been a part of the Spiritual Formation
Groups for a six-month trial period have described a marked increase in the
area of spiritual discipline. One woman noted, "Since I started a group with
one other woman in my church, my life of discipleship has grown 100 per-
cent."

A pastor of a large inner-city church has been developing Spiritual Formation Groups in his church since 1989 because he feels that "they are an in-
dispensable tool of discipleship for the end of the twentieth century." His
goal is to have every member of his church become a part of a Spiritual Formation Group by the end of the decade.

WHY DOES IT WORK?

The secret of the program is the combination of three very important ingre-
dients. The first is *balance*. To be spiritually healthy, we need a well-balanced
spiritual life, just as to be physically healthy, we need a well-balanced diet
and exercise. RENOVARÉ is founded upon the five major areas of discipline
found in the life of Christ and the corresponding Five Traditions seen in the
history of the Church. RENOVARÉ is a program of balance.

The second ingredient is *knowledge*. For most of us, the reason we are unable to become active disciples is a lack of information: how to do the spiritual disciplines. We can dream about being a true follower, imagine ourselves being a committed disciple, but what will we do tomorrow? What steps can we take? What activities can we engage in that will help us grow closer to God? It is as if we were looking across a great chasm, longing for the other side, discontent with where we are now, and yet unable to bridge the gap because we do not have the knowledge of how to start. RENOVARÉ provides the knowledge we need: what to do and how to do it.

The third ingredient is *mutual encouragement and accountability*. Once we have obtained a balanced program and a knowledge of how to implement it, the only thing left for us to do is to begin doing it. Unfortunately, for most of us this is the hardest part. Ingrained habits keep us from changing the way we are. The secret to making the change is the strength found in joining forces with others who have a similar mission. They provide the encouragement we need to get on the path and the accountability we need to keep us there. RENOVARÉ utilizes the God-given strength we obtain from each other.

HOW DOES IT WORK?

Anywhere from two to seven people gather on a weekly basis to study, share their experiences from the previous week, and plan out their direction for the week ahead. This is easily done by following a suggested "order of service" that is conducted by the weekly leader.

During each gathering (which should last between sixty and ninety minutes) one person is designated as that week's leader. He or she then leads the group through a series of opening words, a question-and-answer session, and a closing time of prayer. Within this flexible format, members are reminded of their task, enabled to hear from one another, share, plan, and dream with each other. It is within this framework that the balance, the education, and the encouragement and accountability are given birth.

HOW DO I USE THIS WORKBOOK?

The program itself is very simple. However, a few steps must be taken in order to get it up and running.

- *First, you need to find a partner or partners.*

  How to do this is discussed in the section of this workbook titled "Starting a Group of Your Own." Before beginning Session 1, turn to this section to find helpful insights about how to put a group together. Note: you are seeking to find one to six others who are willing to gather for eight weeks to give this program a "test-drive." That is all you are asking for at this point.

- *Second, you need to educate yourself and your group members.*

    The first two ingredients (balance and knowledge) are currently missing for one or all of your members. This book contains seven sessions that will provide those two ingredients.

    Session 1 will provide your group with the "big picture," that is, Christ as our model and the Five Traditions of the Church. Sessions 2–6 will provide you with a basic understanding of each of the five areas of discipline that comprise the balanced diet, along with an explanation of how they function in our lives. Session 7 brings it all together, providing you with the tools you will need to do a regular, weekly group in the future—if your group chooses to do so. We encourage you to be together for one final session (week 8) to give the regular group meeting a try.

- *Third, you will need to decide whether or not to continue the group.*

    After you have gone through the eight-week trial period, your group will have gained (1) a functional knowledge of the Five Traditions, (2) a knowledge of how these disciplines are weaved into our daily lives, (3) practical experience in each area, and (4) a sense of how working as a group can enhance our ability to accomplish our goals.

    It is at this point the group will need to decide its future. This workbook also contains a Periodic Evaluation exercise for the group to use, and then a series of questions designed to help the group plan for its future. We believe that the program should be given a six-month commitment for those who are willing to continue. At the end of the six months, do the evaluation again.

    Should a group or a member or members of the group decide to stop here, this evaluation and planning section will provide a graceful way to bow out. No group or individual should feel pressured to stay with a program that does not meet their needs. Those who designed this program realize that it will not be for everyone. Even groups that commit to working the program for six months should keep in mind the importance of periodic evaluation.

WHAT NEXT?

If you have decided that you would like to form a Spiritual Formation Group, read through several of the sessions on your own. The sessions may be used by individuals, but we must offer a caution: just as it takes "two to tango," so also it takes at least "two to covenant," that is, to plan and share and hold one another accountable. The sessions can be used as a personal study—we encourage group organizers to study them beforehand—but they will work for you only in the context of a group of two or more.

If you have decided to give it a try, turn to the section titled "Starting a Group of Your Own" to find suggestions for forming a group. After that, you may begin the first seven sessions, through which you will lead your group.

A WORD OF ENCOURAGEMENT

As you begin this program, please keep in mind that RENOVARÉ has no intention of controlling your actions or of demanding that you use this program exactly as we have designed it. We are committed to the Church. This program is our gift to the Church. We are not concerned that you use the RENOVARÉ name for groups within your church; some churches have been calling their groups simply Spiritual Formation Groups.

We want you to grow closer to God and closer to other Christian brothers and sisters. We are pleased to offer you and your church a small-group strategy that is both theologically sound and experientially effective. It is the product of several years of research, of listening to God and listening to the needs of people like you.

May God bless you in this endeavor.

Starting a Group of Your Own

Starting a RENOVARÉ Spiritual Formation Group from scratch, or splitting off from an existing group to form a new one, is much easier than you may think.

The following guidelines may help you put a group together.

1. INVOLVING YOUR CHURCH STAFF

If you are starting a group from within your own local church, the input and encouragement of the pastor and other leaders will be invaluable. They are in charge of "the flock" and, therefore, are very concerned with the programs that the members are involved in. We suggest that you take the workbook and any other RENOVARÉ material to them and let them look it over.

Doing this is not merely a common courtesy; it is essential if the program is to have any kind of effect on your church. The pastor and the staff are ultimately responsible for the programming of the local church. This is in no way an obstacle but rather is an opportunity. If the leaders of your church endorse the establishment of your Spiritual Formation Group—and possibly other groups in the church—you will have taken a major step toward your goal.

If it is possible, arrange a time when you can sit down and discuss the program after the pastor and other leaders have had a chance to look over the material. Should problems or concerns arise, discuss them thoroughly. Don't walk away without reaching a consensus. They may have plans for the small groups in the church that do not currently include Spiritual Formation Groups.

All you are trying to do is get permission to start a group. To date, we have not heard of a situation in which such a request was denied. Most of the clergy and staff people who have seen the program have not only allowed groups to start but have endorsed it and sometimes been involved themselves. Having gotten permission to begin a group, you are off to a great start.

2. FINDING ONE OTHER PERSON

The next step is to find at least one other person who is interested in forming a group. Perhaps you have a close friend, a person at your church, who you think would like to be in this kind of group. Set up a time with that person to explain what the group is all about.

The rule of thumb is this: be enthusiastic but not pushy. Your eagerness for starting a group is invaluable. A positive attitude is infectious, and others will be drawn by your excitement alone. But keep in mind that the group will not be for everyone. At this point you are looking for a person who wants to be a part of a group that will challenge her or him.

Once you have found a partner, you have actually established a group. Many Spiritual Formation Groups are composed of only two people. However, you may wish to include others. If so, go on to the next step.

3. INVITING OTHERS TO JOIN YOU

Are there others who would like to have such a group? Experience has shown that there are many people who would love to be in this kind of small group, but no one has ever asked them. The following are some methods that have been effective in finding others to join:

a. *Using the church newsletter*
   Ask the church office if you may put a note in the next newsletter about forming a new small group. It may read something like this:

   Are you interested in growing in your spiritual life? If so, we want you to know that a new small group is going to begin meeting on (date) at (time) in (place). All who are interested, please let the church office know, at (phone number), or call (name) at (phone number).

b. *Making an announcement during worship*
   Ask the pastor if you may make a brief announcement during the announcement time of the worship service. People like to see and hear from a person about new programs. It can be as short as the above newsletter announcement, or you may want to expand on it. Ask people who are interested or have questions to talk with you after the service. You may ask the pastor if he or she would like to make an announcement as well. This show of support will add to the enthusiasm.

c. *Sending letters followed up by a phone call to select individuals*
   These can be inside your local church, or outside, or a mixture of both. Ask God to guide you to the right people. It is more important that each one hunger for this kind of loving accountability than that they have other interests in common.

   If you are uncomfortable with doing any of these things or are not quite sure if you are ready to start a large group, you may want to form a group with only you and your friend for now. Remember, this is your group. You decide whom you would like to begin working with.

4. FINDING THE RIGHT NUMBER

What is the right number for a group? We recommend two to seven people, though some groups have reported success with as many as eight members.
   The reason we recommend seven as a limit is simply because you will need to be sensitive to the length of time your group will meet. Our experience shows that when there are too many people in a group, either they go beyond the recommended time of one and a half hours or some members do not have an opportunity to share.
   Also, the level of intimacy decreases when groups become large. People tend not to open up in groups larger than six or seven. They may feel like they are a burden or that they will take too much time from the rest of the group. A group consisting of four to five members feels safer for most of us.
   Remember that once your group has started, others will hear about it, and in time, more people may wish to join. Always make room for more. Should your group become too large, you may decide to split and form two or more smaller groups.

5. THE FIRST MEETING—ANSWERING START-UP QUESTIONS

Once you have gotten a group together, you are ready for the first meeting. If you have not already done so, you will need to give a brief description of what this group will be like and what is being asked of the members. Other than you and your partner (who, we assume, has a fairly clear idea of what you will be doing as a group), the other members will probably have some questions. The following questions are commonly asked:

QUESTION: What kind of commitment are you asking of me?

ANSWER: An eight-week "test-drive" and an evaluation session. Share with the others that this is only a trial period in which, for the next eight weeks, they will explore a new approach to spiritual formation. The only commit-ment they are being asked to make is to meet once a week for an hour to an hour and a half for the next eight weeks.

After that, the group will evaluate the experience and will decide whether or not to continue as a group. This will help some of the people who are not ready to make a lengthy commitment right from the start. Most of us like to test the water before we dive in. After eight weeks the benefits—as well as the work involved—will become apparent. It is then that a respon-sible decision to commit to the group can be made.

QUESTION: What will we need to bring with us to the meetings?

ANSWER: If you have not already done so, be sure that each person has a copy of this workbook. You may want to have the workbooks available at the first meeting or get them to your members ahead of time. It is important that each person have his or her own workbook in order for the group to work through the Beginning Sessions.

Workbooks may be ordered through your local bookstore or by writing to Customer Service, HarperSanFrancisco, 1160 Battery Street, San Fran-cisco, CA 94111-1213 or by calling toll-free: 1-800-678-6119.

QUESTION: What is this group all about?

ANSWER: Most of us want to know—in very simple terms—what is the group going to be like? What is it trying to accomplish? How will it go about reaching those goals? You will be able to answer those questions by familiar-izing yourself with the program. By reading over the materials on your own, you will be able to give a succinct explanation of the aim and purpose of the Spiritual Formation Group.

In addition, the following paragraph may be shared with the group in answer to this question:

> During the next eight weeks we will be introduced to five dimen-sions of Christian discipleship—prayer, holiness, the Holy Spirit, service, and the Bible—as seen from the life of Christ. We will also learn about how we can practice the spiritual disciplines that flow from each of these aspects of Christ's life and, between each meet-ing, attempt to do one of these disciplines on our own. We will gather together and discuss our experiences along the way, thereby learning what it means to encourage one another in our individual spiritual growth.

This is a simplified explanation of the nature and purpose of the group. Feel free to modify, add to, or subtract from the above statement or simply to share something on your own.

6. GIVING BASIC ANSWERS TO BASIC QUESTIONS

You may want to cover some of these questions before you actually meet for the first time or take a few moments at the beginning of the first meeting to address them. One of the best ways to do this is to ask each member to read the Introduction in this workbook before the first meeting. This may not answer all of the questions, but it will give the members a sense of what the group will be all about.

Having done so, your group is now ready to begin the first session!

QUESTION: Should groups be made up of only men or only women, or can they be mixed?

ANSWER: That will be up to you. However, we have learned from several groups that the level of intimacy and sharing is much deeper and is developed much more quickly if group members are of the same gender. Why? The more a group of people have in common, the more they feel they can relate to each other. They share similar struggles and are less inhibited in talking about them.

And yet, there is something to be said in favor of a mixed group. Members of such a group tend to add more variety and to have more life experiences and different perspectives to offer the group. The makeup of your group is ultimately up to you.

QUESTION: Can husbands and wives be in the same group?

ANSWER: Yes. But many groups that have done this have reported it to be a mixed blessing. On the one hand, it can be a tremendous way for a couple to grow closer as well as an added incentive in the area of accountability. On the other hand, some people have reported a struggle in terms of what they may or may not want to share. They may feel like they cannot share a private struggle and should try to work it out on their own, thus preventing them from soliciting the support of the group.

We have heard from several couples who do the program by themselves. They are a group in that they meet regularly to review the past week and plan for the next, sharing their joys and concerns with one another. Whether husbands and wives should be in the same group really depends on what individuals find the most beneficial.

QUESTION: Is this group only for spiritually advanced people?

ANSWER: No. While the title may sound ominous and forbidding, Spiritual Formation Groups are actually designed to meet the needs of people who have very little knowledge or experience of the spiritual disciplines. The program uses a step-by-step approach to learning the disciplines, explaining the "whats" and "whys" and especially the "hows."

Does this mean it is too easy for the more advanced Christian? No. The exercises that you will learn are basic and foundational, accepting you at your current level, while at the same time challenging you to move ahead.

QUESTION: What can I realistically expect to have happen to me in this program?

ANSWER: There is nothing magic about Spiritual Formation Groups. They contain no secret formula, and they offer no easy shortcuts. What they do offer is a plan to get you up and moving so that you put yourself in the place where God's transforming work can begin to be effective in your life.

By providing you with the balance (the five aspects of discipleship), the knowledge (the Ideas and Exercises), and the encouragement (loving accountability) you need, your participation in a Spiritual Formation Group may very well be the beginning of a vital spiritual life. God bless you in your ongoing efforts to be an effective disciple of Jesus Christ. Always remember, ultimately the work is God's and not ours.

Seven Beginning Sessions

BECOMING A SPIRITUAL FORMATION GROUP

Discovering a Balanced Strategy for Spiritual Growth

THE LIFE OF CHRIST AND THE FIVE DIMENSIONS OF THE SPIRITUAL LIFE

For the leader: After your group has gathered and is ready to begin, ask the group to spend a few moments (two to five minutes) in silent prayer. When you sense the proper time, begin the session with exercise 1.

THE FOOTPRINTS OF GOD

Exercise 1

Jesus Christ functions in four main ways in the life of the Christian: as our Savior, Teacher, Lord, and Friend. Each of us will experience some of these roles more vividly in our relationship with Christ. Of which of the following do you have the strongest understanding, and in which would you like to see yourself grow stronger?

Beginning with the designated leader, answer this question.

> *Christ as my Savior: He forgives my sins and sets me free.*
>
> *Christ as my Teacher: He teaches me wisdom and truth.*
>
> *Christ as my Lord: He is at the center of all my activities.*
>
> *Christ as my Friend: He understands me and comforts me.*

Allow each member a few minutes to respond.

DISCOVERING A BALANCED CHRISTIAN LIFE

Leader reads the following.

The previous question reveals two things about us. One, we are often quite familiar with one aspect of God in our lives. Two, we are often equally unfamiliar with other aspects of God's role in our lives. This should not discourage us. We should be thankful that God has moved in our lives in some profound ways. But it should encourage us to build on our strengths as we stretch and grow in other, less familiar areas.

The study you are now beginning will help you to identify certain aspects of your spiritual life that are strengths and other areas that are less familiar. We all have tendencies, habits, and "comfort zones" in which we are accustomed to living. Consequently, when we break out of these "comfort zones," we may feel anxious and uncomfortable. This keeps many of us from growing. Authentic spiritual growth will require that we venture out of the "comfort zone" and experience God in new and exciting ways.

Answer the following question.

Which of the following are some of your "comfort zones" or areas where you feel most at home?

a. *I love to be at work.*

b. *I feel comfortable with a group of close friends.*

c. *I enjoy playing sports.*

d. *I love to stay home and read.*

e. *I like to be with large groups of people.*

A PROGRAM THAT FLOWS OUT OF THE LIFE OF JESUS

Have a member of the group read the following.

The RENOVARÉ Spiritual Formation program is based on the life of Christ. As we look at the life of Christ (Sessions 2–5), we will see that he lived a full and complete life with God. When we read the Gospels:

We see Christ at prayer, and we listen to his teaching on the life of intimacy with God.

We see Christ doing battle with Satan in the wilderness, and we listen to his teaching on the importance of virtue and purity of heart.

We see Christ doing his ministry empowered by the Spirit, and we listen to his teaching on the comfort, wisdom, and strength that come from the Holy Spirit.

We see Christ caring for the sick and the needy and listen to his teaching on the importance of caring for our neighbor.

We see Christ reading from the Scriptures, we see him seeking to save the lost, and we listen to his teaching on the importance of hearing his word and doing it.

From the life of Christ, there emerge five distinct areas of his life with God:

devotion to God

virtue in his thoughts, words, and actions

Spirit empowerment in his ministry

compassion toward all people

evangelism toward the lost

RENOVARÉ Spiritual Formation Groups are rooted in these five areas. The basic aim is to gain an understanding of these five aspects of Christ's life and incorporate them into our daily lives. By doing so, we will grow more and more Christlike.

Exercise 2

Question: Which of these five areas of Jesus' life is the most vivid to you?

1. *at prayer*
2. *striving against sin*
3. *ministering and healing by the power of the Spirit*
4. *showing compassion*
5. *preaching and teaching on the Scriptures*

Leader then asks the following question.

THE FIVE MOVEMENTS IN THE HISTORY OF THE CHURCH

The history of the Church has been marked by what have been called "movements," a word used to describe how God has ignited certain groups of people with a particular mission. Once the mission ended, a new movement emerged, emphasizing yet another of these five areas. The following examples illustrate these movements:

Choose a member to read the following.

In the fourth century men and women fled the life of the city to found cloisters and monasteries, emphasizing the importance of solitude, meditation, and prayer, a notable example being St. Augustine of Hippo. The Church was strengthened by this renewal of intimacy with God. It spawned a contemplative movement.

In the early eighteenth century John Wesley and his friends who were nicknamed the "Holy Club" began focusing on moral laxity and the need for the removal of sinful habits in the life of the Christian. Because of the work of the Methodist movement, the Church once again took sin seriously, and the effect of the movement was dramatic. This is an example of a holiness movement.

In the seventeenth century the Church witnessed a new outbreak of the Holy Spirit in the lives of men and women who were called "Quakers," led by the ministry of George Fox. The active presence of the Spirit in the lives of believers became the empowering principle behind scores of conversions. The active role of the Spirit was at the center of their worship, and it propelled them into evangelism, missions, and social concern. This is an example of a charismatic movement.

In the late twelfth century a man named Francis of Assisi and a group of followers abandoned their former lives and went about the countryside of Italy caring for the sick, the poor, and the lame. Countless men and women followed Francis's lead, and the Church's impact on disease and poverty was remarkable. This is an example of a social justice movement.

In the fifteenth century the Church witnessed a renaissance in recognizing the importance of the Bible and preaching. Martin Luther and others provided believers with a hitherto unavailable access to the Bible. A later consequence of this was a new awareness of the role of the laity. The Protestant emphasis upon personal witness and evangelism naturally followed this newfound access to the Scriptures. This is an example of an evangelical movement.

There have been many similar movements before and after the examples mentioned, but these stand out as ones that had a dramatic effect upon the life and history of the Church.

MOVEMENTS AND THE LIFE OF CHRIST

Exercise 3

Beginning with the leader, complete the following exercise.

Each of these movements began with an emphasis on one of the aspects of the life of Christ. Match the aspect of Christ's life with the corresponding movement:

1. *Compassion for others*
2. *Scriptural and evangelistic*
3. *Devotion to God*
4. *Virtue in all of life*
5. *Spirit empowered*

A. *The holiness movement*
B. *The charismatic movement*
C. *The contemplative movement*
D. *The evangelical movement*
E. *The social justice movement*

(Answers: 1-E; 2-D; 3-C; 4-A; 5-B)

GIVEN TO EXTREMES

Exercise 4

While each of these movements (and others like them) was rooted in the life of Christ, as "movements" they were sometimes given to extremes. Within each one there were adherents who overemphasized their particular area of strength. For example,

Have one of the members read the following.

The contemplative who forgets the needs of the world . . .

The moralist who focuses on sin and neglects compassion . . .

The charismatic who seeks the gifts and neglects the Giver . . .

The social activist who forgets to listen to God . . .

The Bible-study enthusiast who feels no need for the Holy Spirit . . .

Which of these extremes have you seen abused most in your life as a Christian?

Beginning with the person who read the above material, answer this question.

The problems that we have been discussing may lead us to want to abandon a certain area. However, we need all five areas functioning in our lives. In fact, this problem is precisely why we need *all* of these areas functioning in our lives! One without the others—or one that dominates the others—will naturally lead to dangerous extremes.

Once discussion has ended, the leader then reads the following.

RECOGNIZING OUR STRENGTHS

Exercise 5

Looking back over the five areas (or movements, or dimensions of the spiritual life, or traditions of the Church), which area would you consider to be your strength area? Which one comes the most naturally to you? If no area feels strong for you, simply choose the one in which you have had the most experience. In addition, which area would you consider your weaker area? Which one is the most difficult for you?

Beginning with someone who has not begun a discussion, answer the following questions.

spending time with God in prayer and meditation

purity in thoughts, words, and actions, and overcoming temptation

nurturing and exercising your spiritual gifts

5 → *helping others*

spending time reading the Scriptures and/or sharing your faith

Allow a few moments for everyone to respond.

REJOICE IN WHAT YOU HAVE, WHAT YOU WILL HAVE, AND WHAT OTHERS HAVE

The previous discussion has shown us that some of us are strong in some areas where others are not, and vice versa. This reveals a few important insights. First, we have a lot for which to be thankful. God has touched each of our lives in some important ways and has given us unique abilities and

After everyone has had a chance to share, the leader reads the following.

talents. We are strong in a particular area for a reason—to exercise that gift as a part of our ministry to the Church. We should rejoice in the strengths we have.

Second, we have a lot of room to grow. Do not be discouraged! It is extremely rare to find a person who is strong in all five areas. The challenge and excitement of the program come when we begin building new strengths we thought we would never have. As we look at the list above, we should look with hope, for growth in these areas is right around the corner for each of us. Let us rejoice in what God has in store for us.

Third, very seldom do all the members of a group share exactly the same strengths and weaknesses. This is one of the great benefits of being in a group: we build upon each other's strengths. When you hear a person say that he or she is strong in an area in which you are not as strong, be thankful for what God has given him or her. What's more, thank God that this person is working with us, for his or her strength will only serve to build us up. Rejoice in the strengths God has given to each of us.

AN EXERCISE FOR THE WEEK THAT FOLLOWS

Leader reads the following.

Sometime during the next week, before we meet again, take a few minutes to write out a brief "letter to God." In this letter, try to recall the first time you sensed God's presence and some of the ways in which God has revealed himself to you in your life since that time. Close the letter by giving thanks for all that you know of God and all that you would like to know in the future. This letter should be about one page in length, and it will be shared (if you choose) at the beginning of the next week's gathering.

ENDING AND BEGINNING
Exercise 6

Allow a few minutes for each member of the group to participate in this exercise.

Passing the Peace: speak a word of encouragement to the other members, making a special mention of gratitude for what God has done in their lives—for example, "Bill, I want to encourage you in your ability to help others, and I thank God for what he has done in your life."

A WONDERFUL JOURNEY AWAITS YOU

In the next six sessions we will delve more deeply into the five areas we have been discussing. In each of them we will learn not only what these areas are all about but also some simple ways in which we can begin incorporating these disciplines into our lives.

Go now with the grace and peace of God. Let us close by joining hands and praying the Lord's Prayer together.

Our Father, who art in heaven,
Hallowed be Thy name.
Thy kingdom come,
Thy will be done,
On earth, as it is in heaven.
Give us this day our daily bread,
And forgive us our trespasses
As we forgive those who trespass against us.
And lead us not into temptation,
But deliver us from evil.
For Thine is the kingdom, and the power, and the glory forever.
Amen. (KJV)

Discovering a Life of Intimacy with God

THE CONTEMPLATIVE TRADITION

THE FOOTPRINTS OF GOD

After a time of silent prayer, open with a time of sharing based on this question— beginning with the leader.

Last week each member agreed to write a short "letter to God." Read your letter to the rest of the group and answer the following question:

What did you learn about God and about yourself while doing this exercise?

Reminded how God has been such a source of strength all through life - how I don't take my time with God as serious as I need to.

CHRIST AND THE LIFE OF INTIMACY WITH GOD

After everyone has had a chance to speak, have a member read the following.

Gospel Passage: Mark 14:32–36

They went to a place called Gethsemane, and he said to his disciples, "Sit here while I pray." He took with him Peter and James and John, and began to be distressed and agitated. And he said to them, "I am deeply grieved, even to death; remain here, and keep awake."

And going a little farther he threw himself on the ground and prayed that, if it were possible, the hour might pass from him. He said, "Abba, Father, for you all things are possible; remove this cup from me; yet not what I want, but what you want."

Reflection Question

What strikes you the most about this passage?

Jesus emotions & his honesty about them - his willingness to submit to God's will.

20

THINKING IT THROUGH

Jesus was a very busy man, yet we see in this passage, as in many others (Mark 1:35; 6:46–47; Matt. 14:22–25; Luke 6:12–13), that he took time out to spend in communion with God. One might easily conclude from reading the Gospels that the central focus of his life was his relation to the Father. He said that he could do nothing apart from God and that his entire mission in life was to do the will of God (John 5:19).

After a brief discussion, choose someone to read the following section.

We see this in Jesus' daily life. He frequently departs from the crowds to be alone with God. He often retreats to "a quiet place" (Mark 1:35) to pray, we are told. In this way, he became a role model for the disciples; when they looked at Jesus, they longed to be like him, to have the same kind of intimacy with God that he had. That is why they said to him, "Lord, teach us to pray" (Luke 11:1). They knew he knew how to pray.

What sets Jesus apart from all of the others is that sense of intimacy. Notice how he addresses God: "Abba, Father." The word "Abba" is similar to our word "Daddy." It denotes a closeness, a love, and a trusting relationship, much like that of little children to their parents. Jesus was not afraid to go to God, to share his fears and his anguish. In the Garden of Gethsemane—at his moment of greatest need—Jesus turns to prayer. His prayer is one of faith: "With you all things are possible." His prayer is one of honesty: "Remove this cup from me." In the end, his prayer is nothing other than a desire to do the will of God: "Yet, not what I want, but what you want."

Jesus was a person of prayer. He prayed regularly, and he prayed often. The busier he got, the more he turned to God in prayer. Why? Because he knew God! He understood God as a loving Father whose main interest was to love, teach, and heal his people. God, for Jesus, was not only a God of compassion but also a God of strength. He turned to God in order to find the strength he would need to carry out his mission. He has, by his example, laid out the course for all of us to follow.

Jesus asked God to "remove the cup" from him, the cup being a symbol of his destiny, which was to die on the Cross. Why, do you think, would he pray such a prayer? Didn't want to suffer - human fear - maybe hoped for another way -

Reflection Question

GOD AND THE CONTEMPLATIVE TRADITION

At the heart of each of the Traditions is God. Jesus is the visible symbol to us of what God is like. His actions and words reveal to us the nature of God. The area we are calling "intimacy with God," or the Contemplative Tradition, is a discovery of the tender love of God.

Have one member of the group read the following.

Jesus went to the Father in prayer because he knew the nature of God— a loving, giving, forgiving God. Jesus tells us that God knows our needs before we even ask for them in prayer (Matt. 6:8). Jesus describes (and demonstrates in his own life) a God of compassion and longsuffering who desires to bless us with wisdom and courage and inner healing.

The most vivid picture of God comes in the story of the Prodigal Son (Luke 15:11–32). A wayward son who has squandered his father's money returns in repentance and remorse, expecting judgment and punishment. Instead he receives a warm, loving, welcoming embrace. That is what God is like.

If we knew God in this way, prayer and communion would not be a chore but rather our inner desire throughout our day. God longs for us, searches for us, and even dies for us—that we might return that longing, searching, and self-sacrifice. Once we catch a glimpse of what God is like, we will want to spend time with him.

Reflection Question

Allow each person a few moments to respond.

In the story of the Prodigal Son we see a picture of what God is like in the character of the Father. How does this illustration of God match your own understanding of what God is like? Very well, this is how I mostly have experienced God — embracing - loving - There have been times of distance — but it was when I was like the prodigal.

WHAT IS THE CONTEMPLATIVE TRADITION ALL ABOUT?

In the same manner as above, have a member read the following.

From Jesus we have seen and heard what God is like. Because of his understanding of the nature of God, Jesus—as we have also seen—frequently took time to be with God in solitude and prayer. It is from these two—the nature of God and the practice of Jesus—that what is often called "The Contemplative Tradition" found its origin.

The Contemplative Tradition is a response to this aspect of God. God desires that we spend time with him, that we create space in our lives to be with him. That is precisely the response God desires: creating space. Our lives are busy and full of worries and anxiety, and our usual response is to push God out of our lives entirely. Practicing the disciplines of the Contemplative Tradition enables us to create the necessary "space" that God desires—and we need—in our lives.

creating space

Most of us live our lives in the midst of jobs and families and responsibilities that prevent us from spending time with God. It is difficult to make that space for God in the midst of our hectic schedules, and yet we are in need of times of solitude and silence, times of contemplation and reflection, times of prayer and meditation. We need those times just as Jesus needed them: for strength and guidance and compassion. All three of these flow from the space we give to God.

Reflection Question

Allow each member a chance to respond if he or she wishes.

Think of a moment in your life when you felt closest to God. Describe the context (what you were doing and the surroundings) as well as the experience.
- College - spent much time in Bible study - worship - trying to seek God's will
- Now - coming back to God in a new way - personal - God is working in me - moving - seeking God's will - struggling w/ saying goodbye - new challenge

PRACTICING THE CONTEMPLATIVE TRADITION IN OUR LIVES

We have looked at the practice of Jesus, the nature of God, and the main goal of the Contemplative Tradition. Now we will turn our attention to the actual practice of the Contemplative Tradition. The following list includes ways in which we can begin to enter this life of "intimacy with God." They might be called "spiritual disciplines" or "spiritual exercises," and as such they are activities that we engage in to open ourselves to God. Each one is followed by a brief explanation of how to do the exercise.

Again, choose a member to read the following.

During the week that follows you are asked to choose one of the following exercises and practice it before the next meeting. Why? Because experience is the best teacher. You are attempting to understand this way of life, and there is no better way to understand it than to practice it. Keep in mind that the following list is not exhaustive; it is an introduction to some simple steps we can take into the contemplative life.

Three simple precautions: First, do not be afraid to fail. The spiritual life is not achieving goals; it is experiencing God. Even in failure we are learning and experiencing new and valuable things. Second, keep your emphasis on God, not the method. It is hard initially, but try not to think about what you are doing as much as why you are doing it. Third, feel free to modify the exercise to fit your needs. In the first session we looked at our strengths and lesser strengths. This particular area may be one of your strengths or one of your weaker areas. Alter the discipline to fit your present need.

EXERCISES IN THE CONTEMPLATIVE TRADITION

1. *Set aside five to ten minutes for prayer.*
   Find a time in your schedule that is free of interruption. Use that time to turn your thoughts to God. You may want to read a Bible verse and meditate on it during that time, or you may want to spend that time lifting up your needs and concerns to God. The idea is simply to stop your busy activities (or not to start them) and turn your attention to God.

2. *Spend five to ten minutes in silence.*
   As mentioned above, carve out a time that is free of interruption. Use the time to be silent. Pray without words, letting the peace of silence wash over you. Two very close friends can communicate without words—try this with God. Simply enjoy his presence.

3. *Read a selection from a devotional book.*
   Find a book you are interested in that deals with the spiritual life. It may be a spiritual classic, like St. Augustine's *Confessions*, or it may be a

Have each member read over the following exercises silently, or have people read them aloud, one at a time. Spend a few moments looking them over as each member decides on the exercise she or he will do for the upcoming week.

devotional classic, like Oswald Chambers' *My Utmost for His Highest*. Others enjoy devotional periodicals such as *Guideposts* or *The Upper Room* or some other denominational publication. However, instead of just reading it as a means to understanding it, read it "with God," knowing that God is there in the room with you! Read it as a means of discovering God.

4. *Pray, using a verse of Scripture for ten minutes.*

   There is a tradition in the Eastern church called "hesychasm," which is the practice of repeating a simple prayer over and over. The idea is to focus our thoughts on God so that God may descend into our heart. A verse from a psalm is an excellent idea: "Create in me a clean heart, O God" (Ps. 51).

5. *Write out a prayer.*

   Take time to sit down and write out your prayer. Write it as if it were a "letter to God." Beginning with "Dear God," go on to tell God your hopes and dreams, tell him what you are worried about and what you need from him. You may even want to confess your sins and seek his pardon. Most importantly, use the exercise as a means of opening up the lines of communication with God. Do not write it as something that will one day be read by others. Like a personal diary, your prayer journal should be private in order to allow you the freedom to be honest.

ENDING AND BEGINNING

Have each member of the group share which one of the previous exercises he or she intends to do in the following week. Encourage one another in this venture. Once everyone has shared their plan, join hands and close by praying the Lord's Prayer.

Our Father, who art in heaven,
Hallowed be Thy name.
Thy kingdom come,
Thy will be done,
On earth, as it is in heaven.
Give us this day our daily bread,
And forgive us our trespasses
As we forgive those who trespass against us.
And lead us not into temptation,
But deliver us from evil.
For Thine is the kingdom, and the power, and the glory forever.
Amen. (KJV)

[handwritten margin note:] Lord Jesus Christ, Son of God, have mercy on me, a sinner.

Discovering a Life of Purity and Virtue

THE HOLINESS TRADITION

THE FOOTPRINTS OF GOD

Last week each member agreed to attempt one of the exercises in the Contemplative Tradition. Relate your individual experience with the rest of the group by answering the following question:

What did you learn about God and about yourself while doing this exercise?

After a time of silent prayer, open with a time of sharing based on this question— beginning with the leader.

CHRIST AND THE LIFE OF PURITY AND VIRTUE

Gospel Passage: Matthew 4:1–11

Then Jesus was led up by the Spirit into the wilderness to be tempted by the devil. He fasted forty days and forty nights, and afterwards he was famished. The tempter came and said to him, "If you are the Son of God, command these stones to become loaves of bread." But Jesus answered, "It is written, 'One does not live by bread alone, but by every word that comes from the mouth of God.' "

Then the devil took him to the holy city and placed him on the pinnacle of the temple, saying, "If you are the Son of God, throw yourself down; for it is written, 'He will command his angels concerning you,' and 'On their hands they will bear you up, so that you will not dash your foot against a

After everyone has had a chance to speak, have a member read the following.

stone.' " Jesus said to him, "Again it is written, 'Do not put the Lord your God to the test.' "

Again the devil took him to a very high mountain and showed him all the kingdoms of the world and their splendor; and he said to him, "All these I will give you, if you will fall down and worship me." Jesus said to him, "Away with you Satan! For it is written, 'Worship the Lord your God and serve only him.' " Then the devil left him and suddenly angels came and waited on him.

Reflection Question

Have you ever had someone come to you and tempt you with some kind of "offer that is hard to refuse"? Describe.

THINKING IT THROUGH

After a brief discussion, choose someone to read the following section.

Jesus' baptism (Matt. 3:13–17) comes right before the testing in the wilderness. This is important because at the conclusion of his baptism a "voice from heaven" proclaims that Jesus is "my Son" (Matt. 3:17). Exactly who Jesus is has just been confirmed, and now the devil will do what he can to destroy Jesus.

Notice that it was "the Spirit" that led Jesus into the wilderness "to be tempted." This may seem odd to us—how could God instigate a temptation? The word translated "to be tempted" actually means "to be tested." There is a subtle but important difference. God tests; the devil tempts. God does not wish for Jesus to fail; Satan does. The Spirit leads Jesus out to the wilderness to fast and pray and overcome the forces that will assail him in his mission. Having overcome them, he will be prepared for the journey toward the Cross.

There are three temptations: to turn stones into bread, to leap off the roof of the temple to see if the angels will rescue him, and to inherit all the kingdoms in the world. The first two temptations are challenges to prove his deity: "If you are the Son of God . . ." Jesus rebukes all three by quoting from the Old Testament (Deut. 8:3; 6:16; 6:13). The devil shows that he, too, knows the Scriptures as he quotes from the Bible to give weight to his temptation (Ps. 91:11–12). However, Jesus knows the Scriptures, and he cannot be tricked. In the end Satan flees because he has been unable to provoke Jesus into sin.

What is important for us to see is this: Jesus remained pure throughout his time of trial. He could have performed the first two requests—he had the power to do them both. He could have accepted the offer of power and fame and glory of the third temptation—a much easier life than the Cross. His actions tell us a lot about the nature of sin and the importance of purity.

Reflection Question

Why did Jesus not yield to any or all of these temptations?

GOD AND THE HOLINESS TRADITION

God cares about sin. The Bible makes it very clear that the people of God are to be free from the power of sin. What is sin? According to the Bible sin is "rejecting the commandments of God." Adam and Eve rejected God's command and ate of the fruit; the people of Israel rejected God's command and fashioned a golden calf; Jonah rejected God's command and tried to run away from his calling. Every time God's commands were rejected, disastrous results followed. Why? God cares about our behavior.

Have one member of the group read the following.

Most of us are accustomed to thinking of God and his commandments as rules that stifle our happiness and simply make us feel guilty. How untrue this notion is! The commandments of God are given to us so that we might have life. Take, for example, the Ten Commandments (Exod. 20:1–21). Each commandment is a call to the blessed life, a pathway to true happiness. The seventh commandment, "Thou shalt not commit adultery," may seem as if it restricts one's sexual freedom. In reality, the opposite is true. To engage in an adulterous affair leads to pain and loneliness; to remain faithful to one's spouse brings true freedom.

God knows this. Holiness is something God wishes for us because it is simply the best way to live. The commandments of God are not given to us to make life a dull drudgery but rather to make our lives whole and healthy. At the heart of God is the desire that we be whole, and sin is that which destroys and fragments our lives. While it seems appealing on the surface—the fulfillment of all of our desires—beneath the surface lurks a poison that will ultimately destroy us.

To put it bluntly, sin is slop. Sin is that which stains and ruins our soul. We are drawn to it and tempted by its whispers of pleasure and fulfillment only to find that it offers a short season of pleasure and a lasting, sometimes lifelong, season of pain. Because God knows this, he prescribes a way of living that keeps us from this seductive yet destructive way of living. Holiness is not a high mark set for supersaints but rather the healthy, functional way of living for all of us.

How have you seen the power of sin (or breaking God's commands) fragment and destroy a person's life?

Reflection Question

Allow each person a few moments to respond.

WHAT IS THE HOLINESS TRADITION ALL ABOUT?

From the heart of God and the visible symbol of the life of Jesus, we have seen how God desires holiness, purity, and virtue in our lives. Holiness has been defined as a life that is functional and healthy and whole. But holiness is not merely the obeying of certain rules. Jesus attacked the Pharisees for

In the same manner as above, have a member read the following.

the mere outward obedience to law while they neglected the "word of God," or the spirit of the law.

Holiness was defined as a way to separate the clean from the unclean people. Washing your hands properly, not performing any work on the Sabbath, not eating certain foods, and avoiding the company of Gentiles (especially tax collectors and harlots) was the way to holiness for the Pharisees. Jesus openly defied this definition, shattering the Pharisees' outward rituals in favor of inward purity. "It is not what goes into the mouth that makes a person unclean, but what comes out of the mouth that makes a person unclean" (Matt. 15:11). Jesus turned the attention away from ritual purity and pointed to purity of heart, demonstrated in unshakable obedience to God (Matt. 5:8).

Yet Jesus could also say, "If you wish to enter into life, keep the commandments" (Matt. 19:17). The commandments are not options. We do not refer to them as the "Ten Suggestions," as if they were hints for building a better neighborhood. Rather, they are the natural outgrowth of a life that is welded to God. If we are in love with God, we will obey his laws. Why? Because we love God and trust God, as a child to a parent, and thus we follow his way. We do not obey his commands begrudgingly; instead, we keep them because our experience with God has shown us that it is the best course of action. This is the heart of the Holiness Tradition: trust and obey. As we shall see, it manifests itself in our lives in many ways.

Reflection Question

Allow each member a chance to respond if he or she wishes.

Why did Jesus criticize the Pharisees for focusing on the outer action and not the inner spirit of holiness?

PRACTICING THE HOLINESS TRADITION IN OUR LIVES

Again, choose a member to read the following.

Once again we have come to a place where our theology must become practical. Since God desires that we become holy (under his terms), it is ours to find ways to enter into this way of life.

We have noted that it is not merely the outward obeying of certain rules or rituals that makes a person holy. When we engage in certain disciplines, we are not instantly holy, nor have we suddenly completed a task that is rewarded by a merit badge of godliness. Rather, we engage in certain disciplines and exercises as means of training, much like an athlete who trains in order to become more proficient at a particular sport.

The end result of the following exercises is a greater ability to obey the commandments of God. We become able to do that which we were unable to do, able to keep commandments we were unable to keep. For example, one of the following exercises has to do with disciplining the tongue. If I tell myself simply to stop saying negative things, I will likely fail. But if I begin with the "inside" by praying for a heart that is pure and then commit myself to watching my words, I have opened the door to the Spirit to begin interacting with me. When I am about to say something negative, the Spirit speaks a word of caution to me, and that blessed split second makes the change in behavior possible.

The end result is not "Wow, aren't I special because I stopped saying negative things" (which sounds much like the Pharisee in Jesus' parable in Luke 18:9–14) but rather "God is beginning to mold and shape my life." The difference of working from the inside out is extremely important to remember when practicing these disciplines.

EXERCISES IN THE HOLINESS TRADITION

1. *Pray that the Holy Spirit purify your heart and mind and then listen.*
   God works from the inside out, and he works via the Holy Spirit to bring about change. Set aside a substantial amount of time (say, one hour) for a deep and heartfelt prayer. During that time, ask God to purify your heart and mind by the working of his Holy Spirit. The key to the effectiveness of your prayer will be your willingness to surrender the control of your life to God. Ask God to search your heart to see if there is any hidden evil in your life, any activity that God wishes for you to cease doing. Then listen. When you have a sense of what it is God wants to free you from, pray that the Spirit will purge that sin—even the desire for it—from your life. Holiness is born in these kinds of prayers.

2. *Respond to temptation with the Word of God.*
   Jesus overcame the temptations of Satan by holding fast to the truth of God's commandments. Memorize those three responses (Deut. 8:3; 6:16; 6:13), and when you are tempted by the enemy to (1) gratify selfish desires, (2) doubt God's power, or (3) seek wealth, power, or fame, respond to the temptation with the corresponding verse of Scripture. Jesus used the power of the Word of God to defeat Satan, and so can we.

3. *Try a twenty-four-hour fast.*
   Jesus fasted in the wilderness to gain spiritual strength. When we fast, we are saying "no" to the uncontrolled appetites of our body and thereby gaining mastery over them. The practice of fasting will also reveal hidden things about us: short tempers, selfishness, inability to delay gratification, and so on. These things can become areas for future rehabilitation. A simple way to begin fasting is to fast from lunch to lunch, skipping dinner and breakfast in between. After lunch, you will not eat a full meal until lunchtime tomorrow. During these twenty-four hours drink plenty of water, and during the mealtimes you may wish to drink a glass of fruit juice.

Have each member read over the following exercises silently, or have people read them aloud, one at a time. Spend a few moments looking them over as each member decides on the exercise she or he will do for the upcoming week.

4. *Two disciplines for "taming the tongue."*

What we say reveals what is in our hearts. That is why Jesus said that it is not what goes into a person's mouth but what comes out that makes them unclean (Matt. 15:11). In other words, what we say makes us "unclean." James also reminds us of how powerful words are. Like fire, they can build or destroy. The following disciplines help us to monitor the things we say and gain some control over the awesome power of the tongue.

a. *Go a day without saying anything negative.*

In the morning, pray that the Spirit will put a guard over the door of your mouth (Ps. 141:3), preventing you from saying anything negative. Be ruthless about this! Do not let even the slightest hint of criticism or judgment come out of your mouth. You will find yourself in situations that will call for an honest appraisal of something (for example, when you are asked what you think of something). Be honest, but do not be critical. Instead, search for ways to be positive about everything around you and be bold in offering compliments as often as you can.

b. *Go a day without saying anything that is dishonest.*

Jesus said of Nathaniel that he was a man without "guile" (John 1:47, KJV), and what a compliment that was! Guile is dishonesty, deceit, speaking in falsehood, shading the truth, manipulating words, double-talk, and the like. Pray that the Spirit will make your heart pure and honest and ask for that "guard" to be placed over your mouth that will alert you to anything that is less than honest and straightforward. Do not manipulate your words; let your "yes" be "yes" and your "no" be "no."

In both of these activities you will find a great sense of release. Our words hurt not only others but also ourselves. When we say negative things, it affects our spirit as well. It has been said, "When we throw mud, we can't help but get some on ourselves." When we say dishonest things, we live in the fear that we will be found out, that someone will see through our falsehood. We are forced to lie to keep the lie going. Freedom and peace are found when we begin taming the tongue.

ENDING AND BEGINNING

Our Father, who art in heaven,
Hallowed be Thy name.
Thy kingdom come,
Thy will be done,
On earth, as it is in heaven.
Give us this day our daily bread,
And forgive us our trespasses
As we forgive those who trespass against us.
And lead us not into temptation,
But deliver us from evil.
For Thine is the kingdom, and the power, and the glory forever.
Amen. (KJV)

Have each member of the group share which one of the previous exercises he or she intends to do in the following week. Encourage one another in this venture. Once everyone has shared their plan, join hands and close by praying the Lord's Prayer.

Discovering a Life of Empowerment Through the Spirit

THE CHARISMATIC TRADITION

THE FOOTPRINTS OF GOD

After a time of silent prayer, open with a time of sharing based on this question— beginning with the leader.

Last week each member agreed to attempt one of the exercises in the Holiness Tradition. Relate your individual experience with the rest of the group by answering the following question:

What did you learn about God and yourself while doing this exercise?

CHRIST AND THE LIFE OF EMPOWERMENT THROUGH THE SPIRIT

After everyone has had a chance to speak, have a member read the following.

Gospel Passage: John 14:15–17, 25–26; 15:26–27; 16:7–15

"If you love me you will keep my commandments. And I will ask the Father, and he will give you another Advocate to be with you forever. This is the spirit of truth, whom the world cannot receive because it neither sees him or knows him. You know him because he abides with you, and he will be in you."

"I have said these things to you while I am still with you. But the Advocate, the Holy Spirit, whom the Father will send in my name, will teach you everything and remind you of all that I have said to you."

32

"When the Advocate comes, whom I will send to you from the Father, the Spirit of truth who comes from the Father, he will testify on my behalf. You also are to testify because you have been with me from the beginning."

"I tell you the truth: it is to your advantage that I go away, for if I do not go away, the Advocate will not come to you; but if I go, I will send him to you. And when he comes, he will prove the world wrong about sin and righteousness and judgment: about sin, because they do not believe in me; about righteousness, because I am going to the Father and you will see me no longer; about judgment, because the ruler of this world has been condemned.

"I still have many things to say to you, but you cannot bear them now. When the Spirit of truth comes, he will guide you into all truth; for he will not speak on his own, but will speak whatever he hears, and he will declare to you the things that are to come. He will glorify me, because he will take what is mine and declare it to you. All that the Father has is mine. For this reason I said that he will take what is mine and declare it to you."

Have you ever had an advocate? What did he or she do for you?   **Reflection Question**

THINKING IT THROUGH

The five paragraphs in the above Gospel passage are acknowledged by biblical scholars as the five Paraclete Sayings. The word "advocate" used several times in these verses is translated from the Greek word "paraclete." Jesus uses the word to describe the Holy Spirit. It originally meant "advocate" in the legal sense, as one who defends or prosecutes in the courtroom. The root of the word means "to call alongside," which denotes the helping character of the Holy Spirit.

After a brief discussion, choose someone to read the following section.

When Jesus tells his disciples that he must leave them, he tells them not to worry or be afraid because he is going to ask the Father to send the Spirit, who will be their advocate, or their helper. The verses listed describe the origin, character, and work of the Holy Spirit. From looking closely at them we get an understanding of the nature and effect of the Holy Spirit in the life of every Christian.

First, we see that the Holy Spirit is the Spirit of truth. He brings truth to bear on the life of the believer. However, the world cannot see the Holy Spirit and therefore cannot accept him. The things of the world are material, and it is much easier for us to accept what we can see. The invisible work of the Spirit leads nonbelievers to conclude that he is not real. But believers accept the Spirit because he resides in them and abides with them.

Second, the Holy Spirit functions as a Teacher. He teaches believers "all things." That which we come to know as Christians we learn through the work of the Holy Spirit. Third, the Holy Spirit functions as a Witness who "testifies" about Christ. The gospel of Jesus reaches us and changes us by the work of the Spirit.

Fourth, though the Holy Spirit functions as an Advocate who defends believers, he is also the Prosecutor who judges and condemns the world. He comes to "prove the world wrong." The Holy Spirit will convict the world in regard to its standing before God, particularly in regard to "sin, righteousness, and judgment." We must always remember that this work belongs to the Spirit.

Fifth, the Holy Spirit does not speak on his own but speaks "whatever he hears" from the Father. He will speak of what is to come, and he will give glory to the Son. He imparts the mind of God to the believer: "He will take what is mine and declare it to you."

These passages provide a clear picture of the role and work of the Holy Spirit in our lives. The departure of Christ meant sorrow for the disciples, but Jesus pointed out to them that "it is to your advantage that I go away." His departure meant that now, by the work of the Holy Spirit, all believers could have individual union with Christ. By this work each believer becomes a member of Christ's spiritual body.

What's more, the Spirit is now given to empower us in our ministry. The Spirit provides us with the ability to experience the abiding presence of God, receive all truth, hear the testimony concerning Christ, convict the world of its sin, and have authority over the fallen world. Christ's departure meant sorrow for his disciples, but it was necessary in order for the Holy Spirit to come and begin a new stage in the work of God.

Reflection Question   *How have you come to understand the work of the Holy Spirit in your own life?*

GOD AND THE CHARISMATIC TRADITION

Have one member of the group read the following.

The Holy Spirit has been called the forgotten person of the Trinity. The Christian Church has always believed in "God the Father, God the Son, and God the Holy Spirit." As a member of the Trinity, the Holy Spirit seems to be the most neglected. We often pray to God the Father through the merits of Jesus, the Son. But the Holy Spirit seems to get less attention in the spiritual lives of many.

This should not be so. From the standpoint of God (as seen through the words of Jesus), the Holy Spirit is God, in particular, God at work in the Christian. What God the Father and God the Son began, God the Spirit continues and completes.

In Michelangelo's famous painting on the ceiling of the Sistine Chapel, God is reaching out to Adam. Their hands never quite touch. The Holy Spirit is this missing touch of God. The distance between God and his people is bridged by the Holy Spirit so that we actually become one with God.

As believers, we are temples in whom the Holy Spirit dwells (see 1 Cor. 3:16; 6:19; 2 Cor. 6:16). We are empowered by the Spirit to share the gospel that convicts and converts, to bear the fruit of the gospel in our lives (Gal. 5:22), and to exercise special gifts that enable us to build up the Church (1 Cor. 12:1, 8–11).

God has chosen to live with his people through the Holy Spirit. He has chosen to empower those who witness about Christ and to convict and convince those who listen to them. He has chosen to endow men and women with specific and necessary abilities in order to build the body of Christ, or his Church. Most of all, he has chosen to bear supernatural fruit from the natural soil of people's lives: love, joy, peace, patience, gentleness, goodness, faithfulness, meekness, and self-control. Without these, the special gifts are like a "clanging cymbal" that makes noise but is of no value (1 Cor. 13:1–3).

The Holy Spirit empowers believers. God, as Spirit, dwells in each of us. It is our job to surrender ourselves to the awesome work of the Holy Spirit and to engage in activities that enable the Spirit to equip and empower us.

Of all the fruit of the Holy Spirit (love, joy, peace, patience, gentleness, goodness, faithfulness, meekness, and self-control), which would you say the Holy Spirit has developed the most in your life? Which fruit has yet to grow?

Reflection Question
Allow each person a few moments to respond.

WHAT IS THE CHARISMATIC TRADITION ALL ABOUT?

The work of the Holy Spirit is at the center of the Five Traditions. As we have just seen, God is at work in the believer in the person of the Holy Spirit. That work moves the believer to pray (contemplation); to seek a virtuous life (holiness); to exercise mercy and compassion to one another (social justice); to study, understand, and witness to the truth of the Scriptures (evangelism).

In the same manner as above, have a member read the following.

However, many of us try to become faithful disciples without the power of the Holy Spirit. The vital, exciting, electrifying work of the Holy Spirit is missing in many Christians' lives. Much of our struggle and failure to live effectively can be traced to the fact that we have not surrendered to the work of the Holy Spirit in our lives.

The Charismatic Tradition reminds us that the Holy Spirit is absolutely essential in the Christian life. The word "charismatic" comes from the Greek word "charism," which means "gift." The charismatic movement has always demonstrated the active work of God in people's lives in ways that make others envious or distrustful. It is here that we should note that the Charismatic Tradition (like the other Traditions) is often characterized by excesses and phonies. This has led many in the Church to split away and form groups that fit their particular beliefs concerning which gifts are still exercised. This is a shame.

The truth of the matter is this: God wants to be active in our lives; to endow us with supernatural abilities; to see us live with love, joy, peace, and so on. Jesus made it clear that the Holy Spirit would be sent so that he might live within us, uniting us in his body. All of us should be able to give testimony to the work of the Holy Spirit in our lives—not just those who are "charismatic" or "pentecostal." Our present task is to find ways to open ourselves to the energizing work of the living God.

Reflection Question

Allow each member a chance to respond if he or she wishes.

Which of the following best describes the work of the Spirit in your life at this stage of the journey? Explain why.

a. *The Spirit has not been a major factor in my spiritual life.*

b. *I am beginning to see signs of the presence of the Spirit.*

c. *The Spirit is an integral part of my spiritual life.*

PRACTICING THE CHARISMATIC TRADITION IN OUR LIVES

Again, choose a member to read the following.

The Spirit is received, not grasped. It is not something we can rush out and seize. In fact, much of our effort will only impede the work of the Spirit. In this sense, practicing the disciplines of the Charismatic Tradition is different from practicing those of the other four Traditions we are studying.

But there are things we can do, activities that God expects us to do in order to let the Spirit begin to mold and shape our lives. To experience the ministry of the Holy Spirit, we must do two things. First, we must ask for the Holy Spirit (Luke 11:13). God is waiting for us to pray for the work of the Spirit, whose working presence is a gift to those who simply ask. Second, we must practice the discipline of waiting (Ps. 40:1). When we pray for the Spirit, we are not praying for an answer; we are praying for God to enter us, to fill us with his presence, his thoughts, and his words. This will require the kind of passion that takes the form of patient waiting.

What kinds of things can we expect when the Holy Spirit begins to work in our lives? While it is true that the Lord works in mysterious ways, the Bible notes several functions of the Spirit in our lives. The following list may give you a few ideas of what we can expect to see happening within our hearts and minds:

The Holy Spirit is able to:

- give us a sense of our unity with Christ
- lead us into all truth
- help us worship God
- guide us in making decisions
- illuminate our study of the Bible
- motivate us to action

- give us the right words as we share our faith with others
- soften the minds and hearts of those with whom we share our faith

These are works of the Spirit all of us can expect to see in our lives. As you go about doing this week's exercise, be sensitive to the inner attitudes, the thoughts and the feelings you are experiencing. You are likely to see God at work in ways you never noticed before.

One final caution: do not expect dramatic or instantaneous results. While there have been many genuine workings of the Spirit that have been immediate and life changing, those experiences are the exception, not the rule. The Holy Spirit works primarily in the area of our minds, shaping the way we think, and this takes time. For example, I may pray, "Lord, give me patience—and I want it now!" While I may desperately want to be patient, as a fruit of the Spirit it will take time to grow and blossom in my life. The fact that I desire to have more patience shows me that the Spirit is already at work in my life, and it is now my task to begin doing things that will bring it to fruition. Genuine change takes time.

EXERCISES IN THE CHARISMATIC TRADITION

1. *Yield to the work of the Spirit.*
   Spend one hour in prayer this week, specifically asking for the Spirit to begin working in your life in a new and powerful way. Remember, you are seeking God. Make no demands; have no expectations. Your only task is to surrender yourself to God. In doing so, you are opening the door for the Spirit to come in and begin making a change in the way you think and live. This may lead to a time of confession.

2. *Nurture the growth of the fruit of the Spirit.*
   Galatians 5:22 lists nine virtues called the fruit of the Spirit. They are love, joy, peace, patience, goodness, gentleness, meekness, faithfulness, and self-control. They are listed in contrast to the works of the flesh: fornication, impurity, licentiousness, idolatry, sorcery, enmities, strife, jealousy, anger, and so on. While the fruit of the Spirit slips in unawares, Paul says we are responsible for living by the Spirit and being guided by the Spirit (Gal. 5:25), which results in the growth of the fruit.

   Set aside fifteen minutes to meditate on the list of the fruit of the Spirit. Ask God to show you which of these virtues needs to be more evident in your life. Then ask the Holy Spirit to begin ministering to your mind and heart. The change will come through sustained communion with God.

3. *Find out your spiritual gifts.*
   1 Corinthians 12:8–11 lists nine gifts of the Spirit: wisdom, knowledge, faith, healing, working miracles, prophecy, discernment, speaking in tongues, and the interpretation of tongues. Some have argued that these particular gifts are no longer necessary in the Church, but most feel that

During the week that follows, you are asked to choose one of the following exercises and practice it before the next meeting. Read over the following list silently, or have each member read an exercise out loud.

the Church is still in need of these gifts. Explore these gifts through prayer, asking God to point you to one or more that might be a neglected gift or a gift that needs to be stirred up (1 Tim. 4:14).

Use your Bible as a tool in exploring each of these gifts. Also, Donald Gee's *Concerning Spiritual Gifts* (Springfield, MO: Radiant, 1980) is an excellent, balanced introduction to the gifts of the Spirit. God may have a desire to counsel, heal, and minister to the Church in ways you have yet to consider.

4. *Read the Scriptures with the Holy Spirit.*
The Holy Spirit opens our minds when we read the Bible, making us receptive to its message. In particular, the Spirit helps us to read the text for what it is saying to us personally, applying its message to our particular situation.

Sit down with your Bible and select a passage to reflect upon. As you read, pray that the Holy Spirit will highlight a particular verse or word that is specifically meant for you to hear. When you have determined the word God is wanting you to hear, spend ten to fifteen minutes reflecting on why it has struck you and what it is you are needing to understand.

5. *Listen to the Advocate when making decisions.*
Romans 8:14 and Galatians 5:25 speak of being led by the Spirit of God. One of the most important and basic ministries of the Spirit is to provide guidance in our lives. Are you facing important decisions? Seek the Spirit—your Advocate—in making your decisions. Here's how: take your concern to God in prayer. Ask that you be given some direction, some insight, some leading, in the matter. It may be an intuitive sense, it may be a word given from a friend that you sense is God's will, or it may be the opening and/or closing of a door of opportunity. In all decisions, test the Spirit by examining the Scriptures. The Spirit of God will never lead you into a decision that is contrary to the principles and commandments laid down in the Bible.

ENDING AND BEGINNING

Have each member of the group share which one of the previous exercises he or she intends to do in the following week. Encourage one another in this venture. Once everyone has shared their plan, join hands and close by praying the Lord's Prayer.

Our Father, who art in heaven,
Hallowed be Thy name.
Thy kingdom come,
Thy will be done,
On earth, as it is in heaven.
Give us this day our daily bread,
And forgive us our trespasses
As we forgive those who trespass against us.
And lead us not into temptation,
But deliver us from evil,
For Thine is the kingdom, and the power, and the glory forever.
Amen. (KJV)

SESSION FIVE

 # Discovering a Life of Justice and Compassion

THE SOCIAL JUSTICE TRADITION

THE FOOTPRINTS OF GOD

Last week each member agreed to attempt one of the exercises in the Charismatic Tradition. Relate your individual experience with the rest of the group by answering the following question:

What did you learn about God and about yourself while doing this exercise?

After a time of silent prayer, open with a time of sharing based on this question— beginning with the leader.

CHRIST AND THE LIFE OF JUSTICE AND COMPASSION

Gospel Passage: Matthew 25:31–46

When the Son of Man comes in his glory, and all the angels with him, then he will sit on the throne of his glory. All the nations will be gathered before him, and he will separate people from one another as a shepherd separates the sheep from the goats, and he will put the sheep at his right hand and the goats at the left.

Then the king will say to those at his right hand, "Come, you that are blessed by my Father, inherit the kingdom prepared for you from the foundation of the world; for I was hungry and you gave me food, I was thirsty and you gave me something to drink, I was a stranger and you welcomed

After everyone has had a chance to share, have a member read the following.

me, I was naked and you gave me clothing, I was sick and you took care of me, I was in prison and you visited me."

Then the righteous will answer him, "Lord, when was it that we saw you hungry and gave you food, or thirsty and gave you something to drink? And when was it that we saw you a stranger and welcomed you, or naked and gave you clothing? And when was it that we saw you sick or in prison and visited you?" And the king will answer them, "Truly I tell you, just as you did it to one of the least of these who are members of my family, you did it to me."

Then he will say to those at his left hand, "You that are accursed, depart from me into the eternal fire prepared for the devil and his angels; for I was hungry and you gave me no food, I was thirsty and you gave me nothing to drink, I was a stranger and you did not welcome me, naked and you did not give me clothing, sick and in prison and you did not visit me."

Then they also will answer, "Lord, when was it that we saw you hungry or thirsty or a stranger or naked or sick or in prison, and did not take care of you?" Then he will answer them, "Truly I tell you, just as you did not do it to one of the least of these, you did not do it to me." And these will go away into eternal punishment, but the righteous into eternal life.

Reflection Question   *Have you ever been a stranger? Describe some of the feelings you had. Did anyone welcome you? Describe that experience.*

THINKING IT THROUGH

After a brief discussion, choose someone to read the following section.

The Gospel passage we have been looking at is a powerful indictment of those who neglect the needy. It may look like a parable in some ways, but it is actually a description of the future judgment of all the nations. Jesus uses a simile ("He will separate people one from another as a shepherd separates the sheep from the goats") to give us a mental picture of what that judgment will be like.

Jesus, like a shepherd, will separate all people into two classes: those who took care of the needs of those who hunger, thirst, feel unwelcome, are without clothing, are ill, or are in prison, and those who did not. The striking thing about the judgment is that Jesus tells both the "sheep" and the "goats" that they have (or have not) been taking care of him.

The "sheep" are surprised at this. They ask him, "When did we see you . . . ?" They remember taking care of the poor and the needy, but they do not recall seeing Jesus in any of the hospitals or prisons they visited. Though the "goats" never went to those places themselves, they offer the same plea: "Lord, when was it that we saw you . . . ?"

Jesus then delivers his powerful punch line: "Truly I tell you, just as you did it [or did not do it] to the least of these who are members of my family, you did it [or did not do it] to me." The clear point is this: the things that we do for others we are actually doing for Jesus.

The bite of the parable comes when we consider that the goats called Jesus Lord. Back in Matthew 7:21 Jesus said, "Not everyone who says to me, 'Lord, Lord,' will enter the kingdom of heaven, but only the one who does the will of my Father in heaven." The criterion for their judgment is not on the basis of their recognition of Jesus as Lord but rather on the basis of how they did the will of God in taking care of Jesus' family members in their hour of need.

We may be tempted to turn this teaching into a deadly legalism, or a "works righteousness." We must be careful on this matter. Martin Luther once said, "Christ did not free us from the law; he freed us from a wrong understanding of the law." The "wrong understanding" Luther speaks of is a belief that by the law (or our works) we can be saved. Christ has freed us from such a notion. At the same time, the fact that we are Christians who have been "saved by grace through faith, not of ourselves, but as a gift from God" (Eph. 2:8) does not mean that we are freed from our responsibility to do the will of God. In fact, our responsibility is all the greater because of our faith.

We are not at liberty to neglect the needy. We cannot hide under the umbrella of faith as an excuse to abandon those who need our help. Jesus told this story to his hearers, and it has been passed on to us to give us a warning. He will expect more, not less, from those who call him Lord.

Reflection Question

Besides the six types of people in need mentioned in this passage, who else might fit into the category of "the least of these"?

GOD AND THE SOCIAL JUSTICE TRADITION

Have one member of the group read the following.

God cares deeply about how we treat one another. The Royal Commandment is twofold: love of God and love of neighbor. As mentioned in a previous session, the commandments are God's instructions to us. We did not create them; rather, they have been given to us as concrete ways God expects us to live.

The call to love one another finds its grounding in God's love for us. God has loved us, so also we should love one another (1 John 4:11). Jesus, too, said, "Just as I have loved you, you also should love one another" (John 13:34). God has shown his love for us, and he expects that we in response shall love one another.

When we look at it from God's perspective, we see things much differently. Each and every human being—in fact, all of creation—is a precious work of God. The book of Proverbs tells us, "Those who oppress the poor insult their Maker, but those who are kind to the poor honor God" (Prov. 14:31).

If we could see through the eyes of God, we would see with compassion. God cares about our needs, our hurts, and our brokenness. He understands our sinfulness—it comes as no shock or surprise. But instead of judging us, he is ready to forgive, to mend, to restore us to health. We are all precious in the sight of God. The Lord desires that we see through his eyes.

Jesus lived a life of compassion for "the least." He mended and cared for the sick, he forgave the sinful, he shared meals with prostitutes and tax collectors, and yet his compassion never undermined his sense of justice. Rather, he blended the two together. His love of God led him to grab a whip and throw out the merchants in the temple. When faced with injustice, Jesus fought against it with a holy passion.

The Bible tells us, "For I, the Lord, love justice" (Isa. 61:8). The Old Testament prophets pronounced the justice of God, and nearly always it had to do with the way certain nations were treating the poor and the oppressed. The Psalmist declares, "The Lord works righteousness and justice for all the oppressed" (Ps. 103:6).

God desires that we "defend the cause of the weak and the fatherless; maintain the rights of the poor and oppressed" (Ps. 82:3). God has shown us the way that he wants us to live: "He has told you, O Man, what is good; and what does the Lord require of you but to do justice, and to love kindness, and to walk humbly with your God" (Mic. 6:8).

Reflection Question

Allow each person a few moments to respond.

In the same manner as above, have a member read the following.

Have you ever had to confront an injustice? How did you respond?

WHAT IS THE SOCIAL JUSTICE TRADITION ALL ABOUT?

The Social Justice Tradition has always been an integral part of the life of the Church. God is very concerned with how we treat one another; he has made that very clear to his people through his prophets and through his Son. When asked which was the greatest commandment, Jesus said, "You shall love the Lord your God with all your heart, soul, mind and strength, and you shall love your neighbor as yourself. There is no other commandment greater than these" (Mark 12:29–31).

In Luke's gospel, a man then asked Jesus, "Who is my neighbor?" Jesus answered his question by telling him a parable about a Samaritan (a people the Jews thought were unclean) who stops to help a man who has been beaten and left to die along the roadside (Luke 10:29ff.). The Samaritan carries the man to an inn, bandages his wounds, and pays for his stay. A priest and a Levite had seen the man in pain, but they walked on without bothering to help. Jesus then asked the man, "Which of these three was a neighbor to the man?" The man responded, "The one who showed him mercy." Jesus said, "Go and do likewise."

The Social Justice Tradition has always emphasized the Church's responsibility to love our neighbor. Throughout the history of the Church there have been men and women who have dedicated their lives to the care of the hungry, the poor, the naked, the stranger, the sick, and the imprisoned. Their impact upon the Church has been dramatic.

For example, the Salvation Army has for over a century taken its battle to the streets, where our neighbors need a helping hand. Mother Teresa and the Sisters of Mercy pick up the sick and the dying in the streets of Calcutta and nurse them to health. World Vision and other mission organizations send food, supplies, and medical care to people who will starve or die of disease before the sun sets if no one comes to help. These—and countless other examples too numerous to mention—are genuine expressions of compassion that result from faith in Jesus Christ.

Often the call to help means more than a shipment of food and supplies. There is an old proverb that says, "Give a man a fish, and you have fed him for one day; teach him to fish, and you have fed him for a lifetime." Social justice involves more than a temporary solution; it involves enabling and equipping people to support themselves. For example, the poor and the homeless need not only immediate food and shelter but also ongoing help to overcome their plight.

In many instances, the social structures of a given society actually oppress people in need by denying them access to or opportunity for a better way of life. Christ calls us to stand against policies that discriminate on the basis of race, creed, sex, or color; governments that deny basic human rights; countries that oppress their people; and societies that inhibit the betterment of certain classes. The Social Justice Tradition has always worked for justice in all human relations and social structures. It is our responsibility as we care for our neighbors.

What are some of the factors that keep people from getting involved in social justice activities?

Reflection Question

Allow each member a chance to respond if he or she chooses.

PRACTICING THE SOCIAL JUSTICE TRADITION IN OUR LIVES

One of the most remarkable aspects of practicing the Social Justice Tradition is its double effect. In the process of helping others, we, too, are helped. John Wesley once said that true happiness comes from helping others. We begin the task of "carrying one another's burdens" out of compassion, but we find that it is we who have been truly blessed in the end.

Again, choose a member to read the following.

There are some important cautions we should consider before we enter into any project of service. In the book *Celebration of Discipline* (San Francisco: Harper & Row, Rev. ed., 1988), Richard Foster notes the important difference between self-righteous and true service to others. He lists nine important points to consider as we engage in any work of compassion. They are the following:

Have different members of the group share in the reading of the following list.

1. Self-righteous service relies on human effort, whereas true service flows out of a relationship with God. Listen to the promptings of God as you begin and lean on his strength to do the task.

2. Self-righteous service is impressed with the "big deal," whereas true service makes no such distinction. Be indiscriminate as you choose what you do, knowing that God is only concerned that you do what needs to be done when it needs to be done, regardless of how big or small the task.

3. Self-righteous service requires external rewards, whereas true service rests content in hiddenness. Avoid doing things for others as a means of getting applause or reward, knowing that the divine nod of approval is completely sufficient.

4. Self-righteous service is highly concerned with results, whereas true service is free of the need to calculate the effects. Do not let your expectations guide your service and do not be disappointed if your service effects no external change.

5. Self-righteous service picks and chooses whom to serve, whereas true service is indiscriminate in its ministry. Be careful not to neglect the poor and the lowly in favor of the rich and powerful. Also, watch that you not neglect the rich and powerful in favor of the poor and the lowly!

6. Self-righteous service is affected by moods and whims, whereas true service ministers on the basis of need. Do not let your feelings, which ebb and flow, determine your actions.

7. Self-righteous service is temporary, whereas true service is ongoing. Compassion is a way of life, not merely an occasional helping hand.

8. Self-righteous service is without sensitivity, whereas true service can withhold as freely as it gives. Listen with tenderness and patience before you begin. Be sensitive to what people really need, not merely what you think they need.

9. Self-righteous service fractures community, whereas true service builds community. Be careful not to let your "good works" become debts that others must repay. Let your efforts be directed toward the building of unity in the community.

These guidelines will be extremely important to us as we engage in the following acts of service. The best way to start your task this week is to begin with this simple prayer: "Lord Jesus, bring me someone this week whom I can serve." This is a prayer that God loves to answer.

EXERCISES IN THE SOCIAL JUSTICE TRADITION

1. *Write a kind and encouraging letter.*
   This may seem a small task, but it can do wonders. Take time to sit down and write a letter that tells someone how important they have been to you. We seldom let people know how much they are appreciated. Perhaps you know of someone who is struggling over something. Write a letter that lets them know you care and that you are available if they need to talk. "Anxiety weighs down the human heart, but a good word cheers it up" (Prov. 12:25).

2. *Spend an afternoon at a local food bank or soup kitchen.*
   Urban ministry organizations are always in need of a helping hand. Look in the phone book, or ask someone at your church, for the nearest food bank or soup kitchen. Call them and ask if there is anything you can do for them. They usually need assistance in areas such as stacking the food shelves, distributing the food to people who come in, or cleaning up the storeroom. A few hours of your time will be greatly appreciated.

3. *Engage in the service of guarding the reputation of others.*
   Though we cannot see it, the reputation of others is a valuable possession. We can guard and protect it by refusing to engage in gossip or backbiting. Paul urged us to "speak evil of no one" (Titus 3:2). In addition, we can stop the poison of criticism by holding our tongue when others are engaging in slanderous talk. Our silence can work wonders in getting others to realize the injurious nature of their words. In so doing, we have protected a valuable possession of our friend: his or her reputation.

4. *Look for injustices and address them.*
   If we open our eyes, we will begin to see areas in our home, workplace, or society that are unjust. Our first task is to examine ourselves to make sure we are not looking for the speck in someone else's eye and overlooking the two-by-four in our own (Matt. 7:3–5). In other words, we must first ask ourselves, "Am I doing something that oppresses someone else?" We should look for ways we might be taking advantage of someone, abusing their kindness, or stifling their growth through our prejudices.

   After a thorough self-examination we are better able to look at the injustices we see around us. We should always avoid judging or condemning or advising people as to their problem, but if we are true to the task of addressing injustices, we will—at some point—need to let our concerns be known. For example, if someone in our workplace is doing something unethical (say, not telling customers the truth about a product), it would be wise to bring this up with our coworker in a calm, tactful, and nonaccusatory manner. Remember, the goal is not to condemn but to see that justice is established.

During the week that follows you are encouraged to choose one of the following exercises and practice it before the next meeting. Have each member read over the following exercises silently, or have people read them aloud, one at a time. Spend a few moments looking them over as each member decides on the exercise she or he will do for the upcoming week.

5. *Take a stand.*

   Is there an issue of racism, sexism, or some other injustice in the social structure that you need to address? If so, discuss with the group what your response should be. If your action must involve some form of civil disobedience, engage in it peacefully, prayerfully, and compassionately. Be sure that the other members of the group are supporting you with prayer and other appropriate actions.

ENDING AND BEGINNING

Have each member of the group share which one of the previous exercises he or she intends to do in the following week. Encourage one another in this venture. Once everyone has shared their plan, join hands and close by praying the Lord's Prayer.

Our Father, who art in heaven,
Hallowed be Thy name.
Thy kingdom come,
Thy will be done,
On earth, as it is in heaven.
Give us this day our daily bread,
And forgive us our trespasses
As we forgive those who trespass against us.
And lead us not into temptation,
But deliver us from evil.
For Thine is the kingdom, and the power, and the glory forever.
Amen. (KJV)

SESSION SIX

Discovering a Life Founded upon the Word

THE EVANGELICAL TRADITION

THE FOOTPRINTS OF GOD

Last week each member agreed to attempt one of the exercises in the Social Justice Tradition. Relate your individual experience with the rest of the group by answering the following question:

What did you learn about God and about yourself while doing this exercise?

After a time of silent prayer, open with a time of sharing based on this question— beginning with the leader.

CHRIST AND THE LIFE FOUNDED UPON THE WORD

Gospel Passage: Luke 24:44–49

Then he said to them (the disciples), "These are my words that I spoke to you while I was still with you—that everything written about me in the law of Moses, the prophets, and the psalms must be fulfilled."

   Then he opened their minds to understand the Scriptures, and he said to them, "Thus it is written, that the Messiah is to suffer and to rise from the dead on the third day, and that repentance and forgiveness of sins is to be proclaimed in his name to all nations, beginning from Jerusalem. You are

After everyone has had a chance to speak, have a member read the following.

witnesses of these things. And see, I am sending upon you what my Father promised; so stay here in the city until you have been clothed with power from on high."

Reflection Question   *What does Jesus do to help his disciples in their ability to believe in him? Why is this helpful?*

THINKING IT THROUGH

After a brief discussion, choose someone to read the following section.

The Old Testament gives hints about a Messiah who is to come. It is a book filled with prophecy about a Redeemer. Jesus, now risen from the dead and appearing to his disciples in the Upper Room, opens the Scriptures and then opens their minds to understand its meaning.

Jesus' sole aim is to show "that everything written" about Messiah "in the law of Moses, the prophets, and the psalms" is being fulfilled in him. The Old Testament descriptions of Messiah described a man who would establish a new kingdom and restore Israel to her days of power and glory, but they also described a servant who would suffer for the people and bear their sins upon his back. By the first century, the people were expecting more of the former (a military leader) than the latter (a suffering servant), and they used the Old Testament prophecies to support their hope.

Unfortunately, their presuppositions made them unable to see Jesus as Messiah. The people wanted him to be their king, and the Romans, seeing this, mockingly attached the sign "King of the Jews" above his Cross. So, when Jesus began teaching them from the Scriptures, he had to overcome those same presuppositions on the part of his disciples. They, too, were in a state of disappointment following Jesus' crucifixion.

It is important to note how Jesus used the Scriptures in the Upper Room. They are a foundation for God's people, a source of divine truth for the Israelites, and thus Jesus points to them as a means by which he can prove who he is. We see in this passage how Jesus viewed the "law, the prophets, and the psalms." They were sacred to him. They contained God's word to the people.

After teaching his disciples from the Scriptures, Jesus tells them, "You are witnesses of these things." He wants his disciples to see that the Old Testament predictions have been fulfilled in him, and now—with that understanding—they are to become witnesses to this fulfillment. It is no wonder, then, that when the disciples began evangelizing "beginning from Jerusalem," they preached from the Old Testament.

The Scriptures became the foundation of the disciples' preaching. This pattern is important for us to see. Jesus asked them not only to witness to what he did but also to point out who he is based on the teachings of the Scriptures. It is not merely what the disciples say about Jesus but what has been said of him for two thousand years that is to be the weight and authority of their witness.

What kind of evidence did you find persuasive in your process of coming to believe in Jesus as the Christ?

Reflection Question

GOD AND THE EVANGELICAL TRADITION

One of the central ways God has chosen to make himself known to his people is through the word, both written and spoken. The Old Testament law, including the Ten Commandments, was written down on tablets and parchment and passed on from generation to generation. The Scriptures have been one of God's most direct means of communication to his people. It is through the written word that we come to know something about God and his will.

Have one member of the group read the following.

The Israelites believed the Scriptures to be sacred and handled them with great care. They believed these stories, these writings, to be the actual word of God, as transcribed by the hands of ordinary human beings. Tradition tells us that when a scribe was copying the books of the Bible, before he wrote the name "God" he must first wash his hands.

The Bible is one of God's chosen means of grace whereby he unveils his wisdom, his love, and his truth. In that sense, the Bible is no ordinary book. It is not merely the recording of history, nor is it simply a collection of wise sayings. It is not only a record of God's dealing with people or the unfolding drama of salvation; it is also a direct means of communication.

Jesus himself is referred to as "the Word" (or the Logos, John 1:1ff.). As the Logos, Jesus is God's clearest expression of himself and the clearest statement of his intentions. Jesus is the supreme Word of God in that through him we have the fullest possible revelation of God. The role of a word is to communicate. Its function is to convey an idea or a meaning. We use words in order to have a relationship with another person; through words we connect with one another. The same is true with God. The written word (the Bible) and the living Word (the Son) are means by which God establishes a relationship with us.

Words are also how we communicate the gospel to those who have not heard and believed. We are witnesses for the person of Jesus Christ, and we use words to tell the good news to the world. Evangelism, then, is not proclaiming our own words but proclaiming God's word to the nations. God is asking us not to come up with clever arguments or skilled speeches but rather to be "witnesses of these things" (Luke 24:48).

In the eyes of God, the written and the spoken word are to be joined together. God intends that the message we speak be his message, and for that we turn to the Scriptures. One of the finest gifts God has given to the Church is his word, passed on from generation to generation. We are the benefactors of the great cloud of witnesses of whom we can read, so that we, too, might be numbered among those witnesses.

Reflection Question

Allow each person a few moments to respond.

How has the Bible influenced your life?

WHAT IS THE EVANGELICAL TRADITION ALL ABOUT?

In the same manner as above, have a member read the following.

The Evangelical Tradition emphasizes two important areas in the Christian life: the centrality of the Bible and the importance of personal witness.

In Romans 10:13–17, Paul explains how these two areas come together: "'Everyone who calls on the name of the Lord shall be saved.'

"But how are they to call on one in whom they have not believed? And how are they to believe in one of whom they have never heard? And how are they to hear without someone to proclaim him? And how are they to proclaim him unless they are sent? As it is written, 'How beautiful are the feet of those who bring good news!' But not all have obeyed the good news, for Isaiah says, 'Lord, who has believed our message?' So faith comes from what is heard, and what is heard comes through the word of Christ."

By working backward, we can see Paul's theology of evangelism as well as its practice. First, there must be "the word of Christ"—that is, the message of who Jesus is, based on the Scriptures. Second, a person must be "sent" to those who have not heard the "word." Third, the messenger must proclaim it, or witness to it. And fourth, the listener must receive the word. In short, "faith comes from what is heard, and what is heard comes through the word of Christ" (Rom. 10:17).

The focus of the Evangelical Tradition is the written word of God and evangelism. Historically, it has emphasized our responsibility to understand the Bible and let our lives be shaped by it, and the result is a powerful witness to the world around us. Paul encouraged young Timothy to "continue in what you have learned and firmly believe knowing from whom you have learned it, and how from childhood you have known the sacred writings that are able to instruct you for salvation through faith in Jesus Christ. All scripture is inspired by God and is useful for teaching, for reproof, for correction, and for training in righteousness, so that everyone who belongs to God may be proficient, equipped for every good work" (2 Tim. 3:14).

The Evangelical Tradition has emphasized precisely the same things Paul did in the passage above. The Scriptures are "inspired by God" and have a pivotal role in our ongoing development as believers. The Bible is a means of teaching, reproof, correction, and training in righteousness. We look to the Evangelical Tradition to learn ways of incorporating the Scripture into our lives.

Timothy had the benefit of hearing and studying the Scriptures from childhood. At what age did the Bible become a part of your life? How did it influence you at the time?

Reflection Question

Allow each member a chance to respond if he or she wishes.

PRACTICING THE EVANGELICAL TRADITION IN OUR LIVES

As mentioned before, the Evangelical Tradition encourages us to engage in two essential disciplines in the Christian life: our personal study of the Bible and sharing our faith with others.

Again, choose a member to read the following.

Many of us may feel a certain amount of anxiety about these two areas. For a lot of people, the Bible is a very difficult book to read, much less understand. As to sharing our faith with others, many of us are often hesitant to try for fear that we will offend someone, or perhaps because we have no idea how to do it without sounding "preachy."

These fears are legitimate. The Bible is not an easy book to read, and when sharing our faith it is easy for our words to be rejected. But this should not prevent us from either activity. By starting with small steps, we can gradually increase our ability in both areas. In addition, the following guidelines may ease some fears.

As to the Bible, it is much easier to read using a modern translation. While the King James Version is an excellent and beautiful translation, it is very difficult for many people to read because the English is nearly four hundred years old. A modern translation, such as The New International Version or the New Revised Standard Version (used in these lessons), is very helpful for those who are beginning to make the Bible a part of their lives.

Also, keep in mind that we are not studying the Bible as if it were a textbook; rather, we are reading it with an ear to what God may be saying to us. On one level we are trying to understand its message (what is it saying? what is the main point?), but on another level we are interacting with a word that is meant to penetrate our lives, molding and shaping our thoughts and our hearts. The best way to make this happen is to read it slowly, repeating each verse several times, letting the words resonate inside of us.

As to sharing our faith, we need to remember that we are only asked to tell others about what God has done, not to convert them. An emphasis upon changing the person with whom we are sharing will often result in frustration. This is because people can sense our true motive and may be offended when they realize we think they need to change. By keeping the focus on what God has done and is doing in our lives, we are making people hungry for what we have. They will want to know more about the God we are talking about. We should keep in mind that people are not coerced but are enticed into the kingdom of God.

These guidelines may prove helpful as we begin practicing the Evangelical Tradition in our lives.

EXERCISES IN THE EVANGELICAL TRADITION

During the week that follows you are asked to choose one of the following exercises and practice it before the next meeting. Have each member read the exercises silently, or have individuals read them aloud, one at a time. Spend a few moments looking them over as each member decides on the exercise he or she will do for the upcoming week.

1. *Meditate on a short section of the Bible.*
   Keep your selection simple: for example, Psalm 1; John 1:1–18; Philippians 2:1–11. Take twenty minutes or so to read it slowly and carefully. Pause after each sentence and reflect on it. Ask questions: What does that phrase mean? What might God be telling me about himself? about me? about others? If a particular word or phrase strikes you, spend additional time reflecting on it.

2. *Memorize a verse of Scripture.*
   Select a verse you are unfamiliar with. The following list contains some excellent verses: Galatians 2:20; Romans 5:1; John 3:16; Psalm 1:1; Ephesians 2:8. Feel free to choose a verse not on this list. Memorization is a powerful tool in allowing the word to have access to our thought life. It is easiest to memorize the verse one phrase at a time until you are able to repeat the whole verse from memory. As you go throughout your day, repeat it to yourself often.

3. *Read one of the shorter books of the Bible out loud.*
   The Gospels, and even Paul's letters, were read aloud to the early Christians, who gathered as a community. Take one of Paul's letters (for example, Galatians, Ephesians, Philippians, Colossians, 1 and 2 Timothy, 1 and 2 Thessalonians, Titus) and read it out loud to yourself. Imagine how the audience of Christians listening to it for the first time would have reacted.

4. *Look for an opportunity to tell someone about your faith.*
   Prayer precedes these opportunities, so begin by praying that God will put you in contact with someone who needs to hear about Jesus. Ask that you be given some means of knowing when it is the right person and the right time and when it is not. When you are asked what you are doing, or how things are going, gently begin speaking about how your faith is central to your life. Do *not* speak in such a way that the person feels that he or she is being judged or manipulated. Simply witness to what has happened to you and let that word go forth in honesty and simplicity.

5. *Evangelize by your actions.*
   St. Francis reminds us, "Always preach Christ; use words when necessary." This week let your actions speak for you. As you encounter different people, pay particular attention to your actions and what they are conveying. The fruit of the Spirit (love, joy, peace, and so on) is a tremendous witness to the power of God. When people see us exercise these virtues, they will instinctively want to know what makes us "different."
   Before beginning, pray for the insight to see certain areas of your life as others see them. By the end of this exercise you should be able to pick out areas of your life that speak well of Christ and others that will need some change.

ENDING AND BEGINNING

Our Father, who art in heaven,
Hallowed be Thy name.
Thy kingdom come,
Thy will be done,
On earth, as it is in heaven.
Give us this day our daily bread,
And forgive us our trespasses
As we forgive those who trespass against us.
And lead us not into temptation,
But deliver us from evil.
For Thine is the kingdom, and the power, and the glory forever.
Amen. (KJV)

Have each member of the group share which one of the previous exercises he or she intends to do in the following week. Encourage one another in this venture. Once everyone has shared their plan, join hands and close by praying the Lord's Prayer.

SESSION SEVEN

 # Discovering a Practical Strategy for Spiritual Growth

THE SPIRITUAL FORMATION GROUP

THE FOOTPRINTS OF GOD

After a time of silent prayer, open with a time of sharing based on this question— beginning with the leader.

Last week each member agreed to attempt one of the exercises of the Evangelical Tradition. Relate your individual experience with the rest of the group by answering the following question:

What did you learn about God and about yourself while doing this exercise?

CHRIST AND OUR LIFE TOGETHER

After everyone has had a chance to speak, have a member read this passage.

Gospel Passage: Matthew 18:20

"Again, truly I tell you, if two of you agree on earth about anything you ask, it will be done for you by my Father in heaven. For where two or three are gathered in my name, I am there among them."

Reflection Question

How do you think Jesus' followers felt upon hearing these words?

THINKING IT THROUGH

After a brief discussion, choose someone to read the following section.

Jesus tells his followers that he will be in their midst each time they gather in his name. Far from leaving them on their own, Jesus promises the disciples that he will be with them forever.

54

Christ is with us when we gather "in his name." The reason that Christians gather together is Jesus Christ. He is the one who has called us to be followers, and it is he who must always be at the center of our corporate gatherings.

If Jesus had simply died and left his followers to fend for themselves, Christian gatherings—whether in a large worship service or a small-group fellowship—would be focused on the individuals who make up the group. But quite the opposite is true: Christ has risen, and he is the focus of all our fellowship. It is Christ who unites us, Christ who forgives us, and Christ who empowers us through the Holy Spirit.

The center of our worship is to be on Christ. It is easy to turn our attention to ourselves, to our needs, our failures, and our attempts to "get right" with God. Jesus reminds us that our power and authority come from him. When we come together and agree on something, we have the assurance that it will be done by God.

The word "agree," however, means more than simply coming to a decision. The Greek word used here, *symphoneo*, implies a harmony that is arrived at only through prayer and searching. Like a symphony, we are called to work together until we harmonize. The unified voice we lift up in prayer comes before the Father through the Son, who has promised us that we shall receive an answer to our plea.

When we gather together in Jesus' name, we are not merely remembering Jesus or the things he said and did. We are actively engaged with the living Christ by virtue of what he has done, and is continuing to do, among us.

Why is it so easy to lose our focus on what Christ is doing in our midst and instead to focus on ourselves?   **Reflection Question**

GOD AND THE PRACTICE OF SPIRITUAL FORMATION

How do people grow in the spiritual life? One major way is engaging in spiritual exercises, or practicing spiritual disciplines, within the context of a Christian fellowship.   *Have one member of the group read the following.*

How do these exercises help us grow spiritually? They create spaces in our lives in which God can begin to transform us. Many areas of our lives have "no-trespassing" signs posted, blocking access for God to mold and shape us. We are often too busy to incorporate God into our lives.

The spiritual exercises that we have been learning about and practicing are God's chosen means to building a relationship with him. The Bible attests to God's interest in these activities: prayer, fasting, service, interaction with the Holy Spirit, and so on. They are God's instructions in how we are to live godly lives.

The growth happens when we practice these disciplines with a focus on God. God loves us and wants to teach us, heal us, bless us, and encourage us; he has chosen these (and countless other) exercises as a way of knocking down the "no-trespassing" signs so that he can begin reshaping the landscape.

We also noted that these exercises are intended to be practiced within the context of Christian fellowship. There are three reasons for this. First, God does not wish us to grow further and further from each other as isolated saints; rather, he wishes us to grow closer and closer as united sinners. The possibilities of sin will always remain with us, no matter how far along in the Christian life we have come. One of the great dangers of these disciplines is that they can lead to a deadly sense of self-righteousness. By coming together as sinners who are on the path of transformation, we stay united as Christ's body.

Second, God realizes that it is only within the context of a loving fellowship that we will have the strength to do his will. Isolated and alone, we are easy prey to apathy, but when we are united, we can better withstand the forces that fight against us. Hebrews 10:24 reads, "And let us consider how we may spur one another on toward love and good works." We need to "spur one another on," and God knows it. That is why he gave us the gift of Christian fellowship.

Third, God knows that we need each other for guidance. From time to time we all need help in discerning what to do in our lives. Are we doing too much? Too little? Are we on the right track? Do we need to be patient? The Christian fellowship can provide some of the answers as we look to one another for help. God often chooses to use others as his means of guidance. Sometimes we are unable to hear an answer because we are too close to the situation. Quite often we find answers in simply listening to others as they share their experiences of failure and success.

God's chosen method for spiritual growth is to practice the spiritual exercises within the context of Christian fellowship.

Reflection Question

Allow each person a few moments to respond.

Of the three reasons we need the context of Christian fellowship, which is the most urgent need for you?

a. *to grow closer to others*

b. *to be encouraged by others*

c. *to learn from others*

WHAT IS THE SPIRITUAL FORMATION GROUP ALL ABOUT?

In the same manner as above, have a member read the following.

All that we have done up to this point has been preparing us for the next step. This is the point when we put it all together. We have been gathering many pieces that we will now join together to form a mosaic called "the Spiritual Formation Group."

The Spiritual Formation Group is a Christian fellowship whose aim is for members to encourage one another to practice spiritual disciplines from the Five Traditions. It is not a prayer group, though there is a time of prayer. It is not a support group, though a lot of support is found here. And it is not a Bible study, though the Bible is an essential part of the group.

It is a group that is focused on what God has done, is doing, and will do in our lives, as we begin practicing the spiritual disciplines. The focus of each gathering is twofold: What has God been doing? What are you planning to do in the week ahead to allow him the space to do even more in your life?

The Spiritual Formation Group answers the question "What will help me grow deeper in my spiritual life?" A poll done at Princeton University a few years ago revealed that the number-one priority for most Christians was "personal spiritual growth." Despite the outcry, there is very little offered in the Church that directly meets this need.

The Spiritual Formation Group (SFG) is, first of all, a balanced approach that makes each of the Five Traditions necessary components in the spiritual life. Second, the SFG provides the necessary materials in order to begin. Many of us are stymied by the question "What am I supposed to do?" The ideas and exercises provide the direction we all need. Third, the SFG provides the strength of mutual encouragement. By joining together, we are able to "synergize" as we tap into the dynamic power that comes from working as a group.

That is what a Spiritual Formation Group is all about.

Which of these three do you need the most:

a. *balance*

b. *ideas and exercises*

c. *encouragement*

Reflection Question

Allow each member a chance to respond if he or she wishes.

WORKING TOGETHER AS A SPIRITUAL FORMATION GROUP

For the past six weeks we have been working together as a Spiritual Formation Group. Each week we individually chose an exercise, made a covenant with the others in our group, attempted the exercise, and shared our experiences with each other. This is how an SFG works together.

Now we are ready to move ahead. This is done by turning to the section in the workbook entitled "Order of Meeting."

The Order of Meeting is a weekly, step-by-step process that gives structure to the SFG meeting. It is not designed to control or inhibit a group but rather is to be used as an outline that will help a group open, conduct, and close the weekly meeting.

Again, choose a member to read the following.

Have each member turn to page 77 for a few moments; ask everyone to keep a finger on the section as you will be turning to it later on.

The first thing a group must establish is a leader for that particular week. There is no single leader in an SFG—leadership is shared by everyone. All that is required of the leader is to guide the group through the Order of Meeting. It is a good idea to decide on who will lead the meeting for the following week at the close of each session.

Opening Words

Have someone read the following. Then have everyone turn to the Order of Meeting and have someone else read the section titled "Opening Words."

Once a leader has been established, the group is ready to meet. The leader then begins by reading the "Opening Words." They help in gathering a group together, giving it focus, and reminding each member of the importance of confidentiality. Some groups choose to read the words exactly as they are printed, and others find it helpful to paraphrase them. Either way, the Opening Words are important in setting the right tone as a group begins.

The RENOVARÉ Covenant

Have someone read the following. Then have everyone turn again to the Order of Meeting and read the Covenant in unison.

The group turns its attention to the "Covenant." This, too, is a simple reminder of what the group is all about. It is founded on Jesus Christ who is our Savior, Teacher, Lord, and Friend. In addition, it is a vocal statement of our intention to do something based on our faith in Jesus, namely, "seek continual renewal through spiritual exercises, spiritual gifts, and acts of service."

The Common Disciplines

Have someone read the following. Then turn to the Order of Meeting and read the Common Disciplines. You may choose one person to read them all or have each person read one until all five have been read.

The third section of the meeting is the reading of "The Common Disciplines." These Five Common Disciplines are based on the Five Traditions. These brief statements spell out our intentions of fulfilling our covenant to seek continual renewal.

The Footprints of God

Have someone read the following. Then turn again to the Order of Meeting and look over the five reflection questions. Feel free to take a few moments to discuss them before returning to this page.

The fourth section is one with which we have become familiar in the past several weeks. "The Footprints of God" is that portion of the meeting where we share what God is doing in our lives. This section includes a number of questions designed to help the group talk about what is happening. No member is expected to answer all five questions, only those that pertain to the exercises they chose to do the week before. However, a member may have seen a working of God in their lives in another area and may choose to answer one of the other questions as well.

Looking Ahead

The fifth section is titled "Looking Ahead." After the group has discussed the previous week, it is now time to plan for the week ahead. Each person is asked to select one or more areas to work on, choose a particular exercise that will help them move forward in that area, and then share their intentions with the rest of the group. The other members may want to record that person's intentions as a way of support.

Have someone read the following.

This time of planning is crucial. We need to offer guidance, support, and accountability to each other, and this can only be done when we have made clear and definite plans with one another. Remember: If we fail to plan, we plan to fail. In order to do the "Looking Ahead" section, we will need to become familiar with the "Ideas and Exercises" section of this workbook as well as the Weekly Worksheet.

Ideas and Exercises

The Ideas and Exercises section is a listing of several spiritual disciplines we can choose from in order to make our plan for the following week. It offers some ideas to help you begin to expand that area in your spiritual life. Most of us find we need some hints now and then, or at least a jump start.

Have someone read the following.

Weekly Worksheet

The Weekly Worksheet is a blank sheet in which to record what you and the other members of your group are doing. Each week you may fill in the date at the top and then, as each member shares his or her intentions, write them down beside that person's name. You may then fill in your own plans as well. This simple exercise is a powerful motivational tool. We become aware of what the others are doing, and they become aware of what we are doing, and in the process we experience the encouragement of accountability.

Have someone read the following. Then turn to the "Ideas and Exercises" Section and the Worksheet and take a few moments to look them over.

Ending and Beginning

The sixth section is called "Ending and Beginning." Its focus is supportive prayer for each other. Groups are asked to share any concerns they might have or any people or situations they feel need to be prayed for. It is helpful to write these concerns down at the bottom of the Weekly Worksheets so that each member can remember to pray for these things during the week. Most groups then choose one or more members to lift up these concerns in a short time of intercessory prayer. When the time of intercession has ended, the group joins together to pray the Lord's Prayer in unison.

Turn again to the Order of Meeting and look over the section called "Ending and Beginning," while someone reads the following.

Closing Words

Have someone read the following. Then turn again to the Order of Meeting and choose someone to read the Closing Words.

Finally, the leader of the week closes the meeting by reading the Closing Words. Just as the meeting began with a reminder of the purpose of the group and the importance of confidentiality, so it should end with the same reminder.

Ready to Fly Solo

Have someone read the following. Then turn to one of the "Exercises in . . . " sections from the previous five weeks and choose one of the exercises you would like to try. Then have every-one turn to the Weekly Worksheet and write down what they plan to do.

Congratulations! You have now walked through the SFG Order of Meeting and are ready to begin working as a group. The assignment for the next week is to choose one exercise that you have not done from any of the for-mer five sessions. Make copies of the Weekly Worksheet to write down what you and the other members of the group are planning to do.

When we meet next week, we will conduct a regular meeting using the Order of Meeting as our guide. We have completed the "Seven Sessions to Becoming a Group," and we are now ready to have a regular meeting.

Also, at the conclusion of the meeting next week (our first full session), each of us will turn to the section titled "Periodic Evaluation." We will use that worksheet as a way of evaluating this group (what we liked, what we didn't like, what we would like to change, and so on) and then decide if we want to continue as a group using this particular program. If so, we will make a full covenant to work together as a group for the next six months.

May Jesus Christ who is present in our midst bless us and keep us until we meet again.

ENDING AND BEGINNING

Have all of the members join hands and hearts as you pray the Lord's Prayer.

Our Father, who art in heaven,
Hallowed be Thy name.
Thy kingdom come,
Thy will be done,
On earth, as it is in heaven.
Give us this day our daily bread,
And forgive us our trespasses
As we forgive those who trespass against us.
And lead us not into temptation,
But deliver us from evil.
For Thine is the kingdom, and the power, and the glory forever.
Amen. (KJV)

Periodic Evaluation

EVALUATING YOUR GROUP'S EXPERIENCE
AND PLANNING FOR THE FUTURE

WHY EVALUATE?

In order for a small group to function effectively and continue to meet the needs of its members, it is crucial that the group go through a periodic evaluation.

WHAT DOES IT DO?

* *It restores vitality.*

    Small groups have a tendency to slip into routines that make the sessions seem mundane. By evaluating the dynamics of the group, it is possible to rekindle the vision and restore the original enthusiasm.

* *It overcomes problems.*

    It is easy for a small group to develop relational or directional problems that slowly begin to undermine the effectiveness of the group. By evaluating the way the group is working together to meet its goals, it is possible to repair some of those areas and lead the group into a more efficient structure.

* *It gives people a chance to share their needs and concerns.*

    The most common ailment of a small group is the unvoiced concern. When the group is no longer meeting our needs, we have a tendency to keep it to ourselves until one day we simply stop coming. The rest of the group is shocked and surprised later to learn that we have decided to quit. Evaluations help us share our current needs as well as offer us a graceful time to bow out without hurting anyone's feelings.

WHEN TO EVALUATE

The following evaluation form should be used after a group has gone through the seven sessions in the workbook and one regular group meeting. After that, it is recommended that Spiritual Formation Groups do this evaluation once every six months.

Some groups will use the evaluation as a session unto itself. Others may use it at the close of a regular session. The important thing is to do the evaluation at the close of the "covenant period" (the mutually agreed-upon span of time the group will meet).

The Spiritual Formation Group is designed for a six-month covenant period. Six months is long enough for a group to get up and running, but is short enough to keep the group focused. It is recommended that SFGs make a six-month commitment to work together, with the agreement that after the six-month period the group will do an evaluation and, if desired, make a recommitment for another six months.

Existing groups who have never used the evaluation should do so as soon as possible. This will help to define what the group is about and where it is headed. Also, while a six-month period is recommended between evaluations, it is certainly possible for groups to use the evaluation at any time.

The following evaluation questionnaire is comprised of questions that will help each member share his or her feelings about the group. Be sure that everyone gets a chance to speak. This may be done by answering the questions one at a time.

SPIRITUAL FORMATION GROUP EVALUATION QUESTIONNAIRE

Personal

1. Given that one of our stated goals is "to become better disciples of Jesus Christ," how has the group helped you in your own personal discipleship?
   a. It has substantially increased my level of discipleship.
   b. It has, in small ways, increased my level of discipleship.
   c. It has not really affected my level of discipleship.

2. In which, if any, of the five areas of discipleship (or Five Traditions) have you seen the most growth in your own life?
   a. the contemplative, or prayer-filled, life
   b. the holiness, or virtuous, life
   c. the charismatic, or spirit-empowered, life
   d. the social justice, or compassionate, life
   e. the evangelical, or word-centered, life

3. In which, if any, of the five areas of discipleship have you seen the least growth in your own life?
   a. the contemplative, or prayer-filled, life
   b. the holiness, or virtuous, life
   c. the charismatic, or spirit-empowered, life
   d. the social justice, or compassionate, life
   e. the evangelical, or word-centered, life

Group

1. Discuss each of the following areas by answering the question under each heading.
   a. *Direction of the group*
      Are we moving toward our destination and reaching our goals, or are we wandering around with no real sense of direction?
   b. *Balanced sharing*
      Are our discussions equally balanced, allowing each member a chance to share, or do they sometimes get dominated by one or two of us?
   c. *Discussions staying on track*
      Are our discussions focused, keeping with the topic at hand, or do we tend to get sidetracked with other concerns?
   d. *Support and encouragement*
      Are we working together as a team, supporting and encouraging one another to grow spiritually, or is there sometimes a feeling that each of us is on our own?
   e. *Trust and confidentiality*
      Are we creating an environment where we feel free to share what is on our heart, not fearing how it will be received or wondering if it will be kept within the group, or is there a lack of trust that is keeping us from really sharing?
   f. *Attendance*
      Are all of us attending the group as faithfully as our schedule permits, or do we have trouble getting enough people to come each week?
   g. *Openness and accessibility*
      Are we willing to welcome new people into the group, or would a new person feel uncomfortable or unwanted in joining us?
   h. *Time*
      Are we keeping within the right time frame, or do our meetings tend to go too long?
2. If you could keep only one thing about this group exactly as it is, what would it be?
3. If you could change only one thing about this group, what would it be?

4. Given what has been discussed, . . .
   a. Should we continue as a group? If yes, for how long should we make our next commitment?
   b. Should we change something about the group? If yes, what changes will we make?

Making a Covenant

If your group has chosen to continue on, the following covenant may be used as a way of defining the terms and length of your future commitment.

1. When will we meet (time of the week, frequency)?

2. Where will we meet (location)?

3. How long will the meeting last?

4. For how long will we continue to meet? (Set the date of your next evaluation session.)

Ideas and Exercises

We all struggle with how to live the Traditions day by day. The following list contains suggestions of ways you can do each of the five areas of discipleship. This list is not exhaustive, nor does it contain laws or standards by which to measure yourself—they are simply suggestions. In fact, you should feel free to modify them to fit your needs.

THREE CAUTIONS

CAUTION I: Don't try to do more than is possible or profitable.

SOLUTION: Use the group as a sounding board by asking, "Is this too much to try to do?"

CAUTION II: Avoid making a vague plan (for example, "I'll pray sometime this week").

SOLUTION: Make your goals measurable (for example, "ten minutes a day") and specific (for example, "for the people on my list").

CAUTION III: Despite Caution II, avoid becoming rigid or legalistic.

SOLUTION: Be flexible when planning, focusing on the interior of the activity, not the exterior.

Remember: "When we fail to plan, we plan to fail."

CONTEMPLATIVE: THE PRAYER-FILLED LIFE

1. Pray for ten minutes each morning or evening.

2. Pray without words (in silence) for five minutes a day.

3. Pray a short prayer throughout the day (for example, a verse from a psalm such as "Create in me a clean heart, O God, and put a new and right spirit within me" [Ps. 51:10]).

4. Set aside a whole hour this week that will be free of distraction. Use the time for solitude, prayer, and meditation upon the Bible.

5. Read a section from a devotional classic. (See the RENOVARÉ *Devotional Classics* [San Francisco: Harper San Francisco, 1992] for suggestions.)

6. Write out a prayer in your journal. You may wish to keep it to yourself, or you may wish to share it with your group. Write it as if it were a letter to God, telling him how you feel.

7. Learn to appreciate God through his creation. Take a walk in a park or a forest or simply sit and watch a sunset. Consider the majesty of God's creation, giving thanks and praise for the world he has created.

8. Set aside fifteen minutes for a time of thanksgiving. This is a time to thank God for as many things as you can think of. Do not worry about intercession or confession; this is a time to give thanks.

9. Practice the art of listening to God. Meditate on a verse of Scripture with an ear to what God might be wanting to tell you. Pay careful attention to the words of the verse: does anything strike you? Turn it into a prayer. Ask God to teach you in this time of silence.

10. Hold people and situations before God in prayer. Take ten minutes a day to lift up your friends and loved ones before God. Do not worry about words; simply see them in your mind—with Jesus standing beside them. Let God minister to all of their cares and hurts.

11. Pray for the leaders in your church. Find a time this week to spend in prayer specifically for your pastors and other leaders. Ask God to give them strength and wisdom and compassion. Pray for their protection.

12. Try praying "flash prayers." When you see someone—anyone—silently pray for them. On a bus, sitting in a waiting room, standing in a line— wherever you are, say a short prayer on their behalf. Inwardly ask that the joy of the Lord reach down and touch them.

13. See if you can wake up praying. Give your day to God, asking him to guide you through each meeting, each conversation, each appointment.

14. Take a "prayer walk" this week. You may choose crowded urban streets so as to bring prayer blessings to many. Or you may go to a park so as to discover once again that the earth is the Lord's and the fullness thereof.

15. Try praying as you jog, swim, or play tennis. Bless the homes and people you pass. Try praying for your opponent!

1. _____ **Ideas of your own**

_____

2. _____

_____

3. _____

_____

4. _____

_____

5. _____

_____

6. _____

_____

7. _____

_____

8. _____

_____

9. _____

_____

10. _____

_____

11. _____

_____

HOLINESS: THE VIRTUOUS LIFE

1. Work on taming your tongue by speaking only when necessary.

2. Try a twenty-four-hour fast to discipline your appetite. Go from lunch to lunch, skipping only dinner and breakfast. Modify the fast by drinking fruit juice and plenty of water. Use the extra time you'll have to read your Bible.

3. Resolve to reply to temptation with silence and prayer. Instead of fighting or running, stand in silence, praying for God to give you strength.

4. Fast from the television for a week. Many have found the television to be addictive, or at least very time consuming. By not watching television for a week, you will be able to see its effects on your life. Again, use the extra time you'll have for some other spiritual discipline or simply take some time to be with your family, playing a game or taking a walk.

5. Be a "gossip-buster." Whenever you or someone you are with begin to gossip, put a quick end to it. Steer the conversation in another direction.

6. Practice the art of speaking positively. Make a resolution to say one positive remark about someone or something for every negative remark you make. Be careful not to get too far in debt!

7. Spend ten minutes a morning thinking on "things that are pure." Discipline your thoughts until they can readily focus on that which is good.

8. Memorize the Ten Commandments (Exod. 20). These laws were to the Psalmist "sweeter than honey." Memorize them in an attempt to make them more of a conscious part of your daily living.

9. Write out a confession in your journal. One of the best ways we can get "on track" is to confess what we have done or left undone. Be honest. God knows our faults and failings—you won't be telling him anything he doesn't already know! The exercise is mostly for us.

10. Cultivate integrity in your speech by focusing on simplicity and honesty in all that you say. Watch for guile and deception, which can creep into your speech in subtle ways. Be ruthless as you seek to tell the truth in everything.

11. Do a "covet" check in your life. Are you "coveting" anything? The Tenth Commandment warns us to refrain from coveting our neighbor's possessions. Often undetected, this can lead to a dangerous envy. Make a "wish list" of all the things you think you would like to have and then turn it into a prayer of relinquishment, letting go of your need to possess, and offer a prayer of thanks for all that you have.

12. Do a "treasure" check in your life. Are there things that are becoming too valuable to you? Jesus warned of placing our hope and joy in that which will one day perish. The Rich Young Ruler kept all the Commandments but lacked one thing: the ability to let go of his material

wealth. If you cannot freely give something away, perhaps it has become a treasure too heavy for you to carry into the kingdom. Experience the freedom that comes when we give things away to those who are in need.

13. Keep the Sabbath. One of the most neglected of the Ten Commandments, the Sabbath is actually a God-given gift for a frazzled world. Sit down with your family and discuss how you can take one day (usually Sunday) and set it aside for rest and recreation. Refuse to do any work, even the catch-up housework that presses in upon you. Resist the guilt and simply rest in God. Allow yourself permission to do nothing, absolutely nothing.

14. In the same manner as above, set aside an hour for "holy leisure." Find an hour this week when you can lay on a hammock, or nap on the couch, or be still over a cup of coffee. God realizes we need rest and will not function properly without it.

15. Write out a one-page answer to the following question: How are Holy Habits developed?

1. _____ **Ideas of your own**

_____

2. _____

_____

3. _____

_____

4. _____

_____

5. _____

_____

6. _____

_____

7. _____

_____

CHARISMATIC: THE SPIRIT-EMPOWERED LIFE

1. Search the Scriptures to discover your spiritual gifts. 1 Corinthians 12:8–11 lists a number of gifts that you may have the grace of exercising as a member of the body of Christ. Look them over, pray about them, and seek to understand them. You may want to read a book on the subject to help you. Donald Gee's *Concerning Spiritual Gifts* (Springfield, MO: Radiant, 1980) is a good introduction.

2. There are other "spirit-empowered" offices, or roles in the church, you may want to explore. Ephesians 4:11–13 lists several positions of leadership within the ministry of the Church. Look them over, asking the Spirit to direct you in your search to know how you can best serve as a member of the body of Christ.

3. Pray for the Holy Spirit. Jesus said that we must "ask" for the Holy Spirit (Luke 11:13). Is he present and active in your life? If not, spend an hour this week in prayer, asking that the Holy Spirit might become a more real and life-giving presence in your life.

4. Spend some time looking over the "fruit" of the Spirit listed in Galatians 5:22. These are "virtues" of the Spirit, a sure sign of the working of God's Spirit in our lives. Choose one of the fruits that you would like to see increase in your life. Pray for its increase and seek out ways you can help nurture its growth.

5. Allow the Holy Spirit to be a part of your prayer life. When you are at prayer this week, ask the Spirit to intercede when you cannot find words to express your concerns and your joys.

6. When reading the Scriptures this week, open yourself to the illuminating work of the Spirit as you read. One of the works of the Spirit is to make the words of the Bible come to life. Avail yourself of this "Divine Interpreter."

7. As Christians, we are given divine equipment called the "Armor of God" (Eph. 6). Look over the different pieces of the armor, asking which one you are currently most in need of. Ask the Spirit to add this piece to your panoply of virtues so that you might be able to withstand the spiritual warfare waged by our enemy.

8. Earlier you may have sought to understand your spiritual gifts. Once you have done so, spend an hour this week exercising them.

9. What "fruit" of the Spirit (Gal. 5:22) would you say you have seen the most evidence of in your life? Make a point this week to let others enjoy the love, joy, peace, and so on that the Spirit has given you.

10. Seek the counsel of others concerning your role in the Church. The Spirit also works through others as a means of guidance. Find a few friends who know you well, and whom you trust, and ask them, "What are my gifts that could be used to help the Church?" From this exercise you may

reach a new awareness, or confirm an old one, concerning your role in the Church.

11. When you go to church this week, really worship! Walk in the door with "a spirit of thanksgiving"; sit down in peace and meditate on God's mercy and majesty; sing the hymns with enthusiasm. Fill the sanctuary with your prayers. Above all, praise. You might find this practice infectious on the others around you.

12. Do a study of the Scriptures on the subject of the Holy Spirit. Use a concordance or a chain reference to find verses that speak of the Holy Spirit—his nature, work, and past dealings with others. Highlight those references that you find particularly new and exciting.

13. Pray that the Spirit will give you a firm conviction of the promises of God in Christ. Read Romans 8 as an aid to this experience. The Holy Spirit is able to confirm our relationship with God as children before the Father. Let the Spirit teach you how to pray, saying "Abba, Father."

14. Read Tony Campolo's book *How to Be Pentecostal Without Speaking in Tongues* (Waco, TX: Word, 1991). It is an excellent introduction to the charismatic life, focusing on the "vital aliveness" found in the Pentecostal churches while at the same time helping us deal with the phoniness we so often see.

15. For fifteen minutes a day this week, wait on the Holy Spirit. Allow the Spirit to move upon you in any way pleasing to him.

1. _____   **Ideas of your own**

   _____

2. _____

   _____

3. _____

   _____

4. _____

   _____

5. _____

   _____

SOCIAL JUSTICE: THE COMPASSIONATE LIFE

1. Write a supportive letter this week to someone you feel may be needing a word of encouragement.

2. If you live with others, help out around the house. This may seem minor, but the chores of the house are usually done grudgingly, and your willingness to do more than your share will be a real service to those around you.

3. Spend an afternoon at a local shelter or soup kitchen. Your help is sorely needed, even if you only offer to sweep the floors.

4. Donate blood. What a wonderful gift we give to others when we give blood. Call your local Red Cross and set up an appointment.

5. Recycle your trash. Caring for the environment is a social justice concern. By recycling you will be helping—not hurting—the possibility of a bright future for the next generation.

6. Help a friend in need. Is anyone in need of some assistance? If so, lend them a hand. They may be putting up wallpaper, or moving, or fixing the roof—tell them you will stop by to help. This is a simple way to care for your neighbor.

7. Write your congressional representative and share your views. Is there an issue you feel strongly about? Be sure you have your facts straight and are sharing out of genuine Christian concern and not just prejudice.

8. Become part of a prison ministry. Your local church should know of some existing prison ministries in your area. Go with them for a day and spend some time visiting with an inmate. These people think the world has no need of them. Jesus told us that when we visit them, we are visiting him (Matt. 25).

9. Address an injustice with compassion. Is someone being treated unfairly? Do not be silent when your words may very well make a difference.

10. Practice the service of hiddenness. Do a kind deed for someone (say, shoveling a sidewalk or picking up litter along a highway) without anyone noticing it or giving you the credit.

11. Serve others with your words. Protect people's reputations and speak well of others as a means of serving them. Kind words are great deeds.

12. Serve others by letting them have "space." We sometimes devour people, or consume their time, or usurp their freedom with our expectations. Make a concerted effort to give people free time and space. Ask them what they want to do or if they want to be alone.

13. Serve others by letting others serve you. Are you guilty of not letting other people do things for you? This is a sin. It is a gift to others to let them serve you; do not deny them this joy.

14. Read *The Politics of Jesus* (Grand Rapids, MI: Eerdmans, 1972) by John Howard Yoder as a way of forcing yourself to ask the hard justice questions. You might also try Donald Kraybill's book, *The Upside-Down Kingdom* (Scottdale, PA: Herald, 1990). You may not agree with everything these authors say, but they should stimulate your thinking.

15. Write a one-page response this week to the following question: What is the most pressing social justice issue today, and what position should the Christian take regarding it? Share your paper with the other members of your Spiritual Formation Group.

1. _____ **Ideas of your own**

_____

2. _____

_____

3. _____

_____

4. _____

_____

5. _____

_____

6. _____

_____

7. _____

_____

8. _____

_____

9. _____

_____

EVANGELICAL: THE WORD-CENTERED LIFE

1. Read the Bible for fifteen minutes a day. Choose a method of reading (for example, a chapter a day or selections from a devotional book) and stick to it. Let the Bible influence your day.

2. Read a chapter of the Bible before falling asleep. This is a nice way to end the day. If you live with a spouse or roommate, you may want to read it aloud with that person.

3. Meditate on a psalm once a day. The psalms are wonderful prayers that are excellent means of communing with God. Let the words of the psalm be your words. Read them slowly, over and over, until they become your prayers.

4. Memorize a verse or passage of Scripture. Some people like to memorize "theme" verses (for example, verses that relate to the power of God). Choose one verse, or even two or three, and be able to repeat it back to your group from memory during the next meeting.

5. Study the Bible. Use a Bible that has "helps" or study notes or get a good commentary and look deeply into a passage, a chapter, or a book of the Bible.

6. Write out a favorite verse on an index card and put it (1) on your mirror, (2) on the dashboard of your car, or (3) somewhere you frequent during the day. This will help you to see it several times, making it a more available source of inspiration.

7. Keep track in a journal of what you are learning from your reading of the Bible.

8. Share your faith with a relative or close friend. So often we neglect to talk about our faith with our friends and family, but how important that can be!

9. Make a real effort to reach others with the message of Christ. When you are talking with someone, steer the conversation to things of ultimate importance (life, death, meaning). Ask the person how he or she feels about all of this. If the door shuts, politely drop it. But if you sense a yearning to hear your thoughts, freely share what Christ means to you.

10. Invite a friend to church. It is said that the major reason people become members of a church is because someone invited them! Are there people you know who are unchurched? Invite them to go with you this Sunday.

11. Be a "discipler" for a new Christian. If you have been a Christian for some time, you can do a great service to a new Christian who needs a model—and possibly some answers. Don't hide your light! You can do this by keeping your eye out for young believers and asking them if they would like to get together sometime to study the Bible and pray together.

12. Listen to the Bible on tape. You may not have the money, but the audio-cassettes of the Bible are a wonderful tool to help you learn the Scrip-

tures. Your church, or a friend, may have a set that you can borrow. Listen to them in your car, or on a headset during a work break, or before falling asleep. The oral tradition of the Bible is a great way to hear and understand the word of the Scriptures.

13. For one week record your answer to the following question: How has my reading of the Bible influenced the way I relate to my family?

14. Try to develop a genuine friendship with a non-Christian at work or in the neighborhood.

15. This week become acquainted with one of your neighbors. Simple friendliness can often afford opportunities to share God's goodness.

Ideas of your own

1. _____

2. _____

3. _____

4. _____

5. _____

6. _____

7. _____

8. _____

9. _____

Order of Meeting

I. OPENING WORDS

Welcome to the RENOVARÉ (or other chosen name for the group) Spiritual Formation Group. May God's Holy Spirit bless us, and may we find fellowship and encouragement during this time together.

Remember, we gather together with one purpose in mind—to become better disciples of Jesus Christ. We do this by encouraging one another to keep his commands, which, as he said, is how we love him (John 14:23–24). Through the grace of mutual accountability, our aim is to inspire one another to love and good works.

Please keep in mind that everything that is said here is to be held in confidence. Only then can we feel free enough to share openly and honestly. All hopes and dreams, all fears and failures—even our joys and successes are to be kept within these walls. This is how we help each other.

Before you begin, spend a few moments in silence. Then the leader for the week begins by reading the following.

II. THE COVENANT

In utter dependence upon Jesus Christ as
my everliving Savior, Teacher, Lord, and Friend,
I will seek continual renewal through:

- spiritual exercises,
- spiritual gifts, and
- acts of service.

Read the following covenant as a group in unison.

III. THE COMMON DISCIPLINES

Beginning with the leader, take turns reading until all five disciplines have been read.

1. I will set aside time regularly for prayer, meditation, and spiritual reading and will seek to practice the presence of God.

2. By God's grace, I will strive mightily against sin, and will do deeds of love and mercy that lead to righteousness.

3. I will seek the gifts of the Holy Spirit, nurturing the fruit and experiencing the joy and power of the Spirit.

4. I will seek to serve others everywhere I can and will work for justice in all human relationships and social structures.

5. I will study the Scriptures regularly and share my faith with others as God leads.

IV. THE FOOTPRINTS OF GOD

Beginning with the designated leader, share each of your experiences from the previous week. The following questions may be used to help focus the discussion. As time permits, we encourage everyone to answer at least the first question under each number in this section.

1. In what ways did God make his presence known to you since our last meeting? What experiences of prayer, meditation, and spiritual reading has God given you? What difficulties or frustrations did you encounter? What joys and delights?

2. What temptations did you face since our last meeting? How did you respond? Which spiritual disciplines did God use to lead you further into holiness of heart and life?

3. Have you sensed any influence or work of the Holy Spirit since our last meeting? What spiritual gifts did the Spirit enable you to exercise? What was the outcome? What fruit of the Spirit would you like to see increase in your life? Which disciplines might be useful in this effort?

4. What opportunities did God give you to serve others since our last meeting? How did you respond? Did you encounter injustice to or oppression of others? Were you able to work for justice and shalom?

5. In what ways did you encounter Christ in your reading of the Scripture since our last meeting? How has the Bible shaped the way you think and live? Did God provide an opportunity for you to share your faith with someone? How did you respond?

V. LOOKING AHEAD

Which area or areas would you like to work on this week? What specific exercises would you like to try?

Beginning with the designated leader, allow time for each member to share his or her intentions for the upcoming week. The following questions may be used as guidelines for your planning. Use copies of the Weekly Worksheet found on page 81 of this workbook to write down what you and the other members have chosen to do during the upcoming week. Writing them down will help you to remember what others are doing as well as give you a chance to pray for them during the week.

VI. ENDING AND BEGINNING

Our Father, who art in heaven,
Hallowed be Thy name.
Thy kingdom come,
Thy will be done,
On earth, as it is in heaven.
Give us this day our daily bread,
And forgive us our trespasses
As we forgive those who trespass against us.
And lead us not into temptation,
But deliver us from evil.
For Thine is the kingdom, and the power, and the glory forever.
Amen. (KJV)

After each person has had a chance to speak, ask if anyone in the group has a particular need or knows of situations that should be prayed for. Again, use the Weekly Worksheet to write down the prayer concerns that have been mentioned so that you can pray for these concerns throughout the week. Choose someone in the group to pray over these concerns. After the person has prayed, join together in praying the Lord's Prayer.

VII. CLOSING WORDS

At the conclusion of the Lord's Prayer, the designated leader ends the meeting by reading the Closing Words.

Please remember that what you have said here and what you have heard here was spoken in confidence and should remain here when you leave. May the love, the peace, and power of God be with us all this week as we endeavor to do his will. Amen.

For future use, you may choose to remove these Order of Meeting pages for more handy reference.

Weekly Worksheet

"And let us consider how we may spur one another on toward love and good deeds." (Heb. 10:24)

PLAN FOR THIS WEEK   Date _____
Area of Discipleship

You do not have to choose exercises from all of the areas each week.

_____ *Contemplative*

_____

_____ *Holiness*

_____

_____ *Charismatic*

_____

_____ *Social Justice*

_____

_____ *Evangelical*

_____

This page may be photocopied for local use.

Plans for Other Members of the Group

Name _____   _____

                           _____

                           _____

Name _____   _____

                           _____

                           _____

Name _____   _____

                           _____

                           _____

Name _____   _____

                           _____

                           _____

"Cast your anxieties upon God because he cares for you." (1 Pet. 5:7)

Prayer concerns: _____

_____

_____

_____

Other notes: _____

_____

_____

_____

This page may be photocopied for local use.

- 5-15-95

- School in Rockingham - Temple Christian School
- Kim - goals in life / God's will
- Finding home in Durham - Lisa
- Terry's brother Don - Angioplasty & becoming a Christian
        - Direction from Lord
- Beth - "fretting" cycle - remaking Father's death

6-10-95

- Paul's mother-in-law

(June 19 Mon)

- Uncle of Beth - Heart By Pass on Thsday

- Terry's son - Paul had surgery

- Billy & Lisa

- Janet's friend moving from church - grieving
    (moving away from Janet)

☒ Steve McElroy - moving to Pinehurst

- Jack Hunter

-